The Girl in the Yellow Pantsuit

Essays on
Politics, History, and Culture

BECCA BALINT

§

The Girl in the Yellow Pantsuit

Essays on
Politics, History, and Culture

GREEN WRITERS PRESS   *Brattleboro, Vermont*

Printed in the United States

10 9 8 7 6 5 4 3 2 1

Green Writers Press is a Vermont-based publisher whose mission
is to spread a message of hope and renewal through the words and
images we publish. Throughout we will adhere to our commitment to
preserving and protecting the natural resources of the earth. To that
end, a percentage of our proceeds will be donated to environmental
activist groups. Green Writers Press gratefully acknowledges support
from individual donors, friends, and readers to help support the
environment and our publishing initiative.

GReen
wriTers
press

Giving Voice to Writers & Artists Who Will Make the World a Better Place
Green Writers Press | West Brattleboro, Vermont
www.greenwriterspress.com

Library of Congress Cataloging-in-Publication Data available upon request.

ISBN: 978-1-950584-37-6

"Don't Hesitate" by Mary Oliver. Reprinted by the permission
of The Charlotte Sheedy Literary Agency as agent for the author.
Copyright © NW Orchard LLC 2010 with permission of Bill Reichblum.

PRINTED ON PAPER WITH PULP THAT COMES FROM FSC-CERTIFIED FORESTS, MANAGED FORESTS
THAT GUARANTEE RESPONSIBLE ENVIRONMENTAL, SOCIAL, AND ECONOMIC PRACTICES.

To my beloved spouse, Elizabeth, and our two clever and eccentric children, Abraham and Sarah. I simply couldn't do all the things I do without your love and support.

We must reject not only the stereotypes others hold of us, but also the stereotypes we hold of ourselves.

—SHIRLEY CHISHOLM, *first Black woman to serve in Congress, representing New York State's 12th congressional district for seven terms, 1969–83*

Contents

❦

Foreword

§

By Retired Vermont Supreme Court
Justice Marilyn Skoglund

T HIS BOOK should come with a packet of sticky notes so the reader can mark the pages of the essays that will be revisited often when a boost is needed. Becca is not trying to sell you on her belief systems or philosophies; she only invites us to think about the ideas she explores. And her explorations are sometimes very funny, sometimes poignant, always thoughtful, well researched, and unsullied by hidden agendas.

Drawing from columns that she began writing for the *Brattleboro Reformer* newspaper back in 2012, she shares her thoughts on many disparate topics: from empathy, community, and parenthood, to bullying, the murder of Jamal Khashoggi, and racism. Many of her essays are grounded in serious academic studies. To her themes she adds descriptions of research into Dr. Martin Seligman's work identifying positive psychological traits; a discussion of mirror neurons as the basis of human empathy; the work of Professor Laura Kubzansky from the Harvard School of Public Health on the effect of negative emotions on health; and many other researchers who provide a solid base for her reflections.

And she can write. Sometimes she illustrates her stories with wit and humor, as when she writes: "my kids enjoy teasing each other so much that I feel like I'm watching Elizabethan bear baiting." Even in her humor, she reveals her familiarity with a huge mélange of historical knowledge. Sometimes her best writing rests on the briefest of commentary, and sometimes her words strike deep, as in her discussion of racial prejudice and vicious bigotry.

And when you think you know where she's going in a story about American's negative attitudes towards the French, and you find yourself learning about France's kinder, more informed treatment of the homeless—but not until she ruminates about crusty French bread, weapons of mass destruction, and Jerry Lewis's inane comedies.

In "A Tale of Four Mowers," she celebrates her neighbors' generosity. Frankly, I would have quit trying to subdue my lawn after the first borrowed lawnmower died, and resorted to doing a semi-controlled burn of the grass. But she persists until she accomplishes what she started, all the while extolling the virtues of her neighborhood. Yet, in another piece, she talks about her father's distrust of neighbors because of his father's murder by the Nazis.

The range of her essays assures us that she is well aware that everything is not sweetness and light in our world. She examines political deceit and the stigma of mental illness with the same thoughtfulness that she brings to community and friendships. One of my favorite essays encourages us to celebrate flashes of greatness wherever we can, using the life of Hector "Macho" Camacho's brilliant career in the boxing ring and balancing it against his sometimes unsavory, troubled personal life.

Becca shares a lot about herself in this volume. We know she has never once regretted sending a thank-you note, that her spirituality resides in the natural world, that she knows how to make a campfire in a downpour. But we also glean the scope of her intellect, compassion, and humanity. What you won't find in this volume is apathy. That she cares deeply is clear. That she thinks deeply is evident. This book is Becca exhorting us to balance our strong convictions with a healthy curiosity about what we might be getting wrong. And to think harder.

Introduction

§

WHEN I FIRST CONSIDERED turning my weekly columns into a compilation in book form, I thought the project would be straightforward. All I'd need to do was pick some of my favorites, do some careful editing, put them into some kind of order, and—*voilà!*—that would be that. Oh, how wrong I was! I hadn't stopped to think about how difficult it would be to choose the columns or how I'd *feel* about those columns now, sometimes many years after I'd initially written them.

It also took some courage to start this project. When I initially sat down with my editor to begin work on this compilation of editorials, I confessed, "I'm excited about this project, but I'm also feeling vulnerable and uncomfortable." He smiled and said something like, "I bet you are. We're essentially curating your life and ideas for the general public. This is all about you."

He told me to think of it as "Intro to Becca 101"—my columns would provide insight into who I am and what drives me.

That is partially true, but these columns are also snapshots in time. Each one reflects my thoughts about a particular issue at a specific time in my life and in my evolution as a writer. Although my core values and beliefs haven't changed, my ideas have shifted as I have learned more about myself—and as the world has changed. I am not the same writer I was ten years ago. These columns would be different if I wrote them today. That realization meant I needed to accept what I wrote at that time. I also needed to accept that I would have moments of unease; I see the mistakes and where I missed the mark. Obviously, that's uncomfortable. What's more, I doubted that anyone would want to read this compilation of columns.

But that's why I called this book *The Girl in the Yellow Pantsuit*. That column is about showing others who you are—being truly vulnerable—even when its uncomfortable. Writing an editorial column for years is an exercise in public exposure—but naming the discomfort also helps to release the anxiety.

These columns have been a way for me to expand the arena in which I get to give voice to something or shine a light on particular issues. Each essay started from an idea that was kicking around in my head but then evolved into a conversation with my broader community. It's been an interesting transformation to witness; my editorials begin as soliloquies but end up as dialogues and group discussions with neighbors, friends, and constituents. I'm grateful I've had the opportunity to have this impact.

This is a book of columns, a collection of ideas. But it's also a reflection of an eight-year arc—my journey towards finding my writer's voice and rediscovering and owning my life's purpose. Instead of a "coming of age" story, it is more of a "claiming of place" story. It's a story about stepping into my place and fully embracing the impact I can and do have on those around me.

We all have impact, both intentional and unintentional. But we seldom take the time to reflect on that impact. My columns have given me the wonderful gift of reflection. I understand my community and my state—and my place within those two spheres—very differently now than I did before I started writing my column. And I know the column, and the constant feedback about it, has made me a better representative of my constituents.

I've always been curious and opinionated, and I'm fortunate that my friends and family encouraged this in me. When friend and talented writer Becky Karush suggested I submit some work to the *Brattleboro Reformer* and become a weekly columnist, I was intrigued—but also intimidated by the prospect of writing an editorial every single week. She said, "You've got a lot of ideas, Becca. And I think you could use a bigger platform." I was flattered that she thought I'd be able to do the job, and I was grateful that Bob Audette, one of the editors at the *Reformer* at the time, gave me a shot at it. I've written a lot of columns since then and (by my rough count) nearly a quarter million words. But it all started with a nudge from Becky and Bob.

In retrospect, writing an op-ed column feels completely right. When I was still a high school student I won a leadership award, and a reporter interviewed me for our local newspaper. The reporter asked my seventeen-year-old self what I thought I would do with my life. Fortunately, I know what I said because my mom saved the newspaper clipping and whipped out the yellowing paper to show me when I first ran for office. I responded that I hoped to teach, to write, and to maybe someday run for office. "Whatever I do," I told the reporter, "I want to work to improve people's lives." Even as a teenager, I was so very clear about what I wanted my life to embody.

At seventeen I knew I was called to politics, but I also knew I was gay. I didn't know of any "out" gay politicians except for San Francisco city council member Harvey Milk. And he'd been assassinated. It didn't seem like running for office as an openly gay woman would ever be a possibility in my lifetime. I also had no political role models in my family or extended family. There wasn't a single person I could point to on either side of my family who'd ever been in politics in any way. And my dad's immigrant family and my mom's working-class family had no political connections or wealth. It seemed like an impossibility, so I ignored the call.

Instead, I built a career teaching history and social studies, which provided me with an outlet for my creativity, my curiosity, and my opinions. My classroom was infused with art, theater, and hilarity. My students were up for just about anything, and we laughed and learned a great deal together.

But I still felt like I wasn't doing the thing I was called to do. The toughest part for me was that I didn't have even a tiny notion of where to begin. And I didn't think that, in my mid-forties, it would be possible to change the direction of my life. I'm indebted to my spouse, Elizabeth Wohl, and my mentor and coach, Laura Coyle, for pushing me to do the thing I was called to do—despite my fears and misgivings.

When I first left teaching to stay home to raise our kids, I really struggled. Some people feel completely fulfilled by raising children as a primary purpose; I didn't, despite it being extremely important. I knew that some of my friends found it very rewarding and challenging, something they felt called to do. I felt guilty because I didn't feel this way. I was a loving and engaged mom, and I knew I had a broader purpose. I felt lost for several years.

I had one master's degree in education and another one in history, and I didn't know what to do next. I had one harebrained career scheme after another: making genuine Vermont switchel; running a donut shop; publishing children's books; manufacturing "elbow" mittens—all things that require business experience, something I absolutely didn't have. I attended career workshops and talked to friends about what I should do for the next chapter of my life. I applied to a principal certification program and also considered going back to school for my PhD in history. None of it felt right. This overwhelming feeling of being stuck would sometimes come out as impatience, other times as anger or depression.

A CHANCE MEETING at a New Year's Eve party on the last day of 2011 marked a new beginning for me. A friend's wife introduced me to a woman who would become my longtime mentor and coach, Laura Coyle, who worked through the Co-Active Training Institute. We hit it off easily, first while sledding and laughing, and then later while singing and playing guitar. Now, more than ten years later, she is still my mentor and coach.

When I look back through my notes from my first few sessions with Laura, one of the things I notice is that I genuinely believed that the time had passed for me to run for office. My spouse's career, my young children, my status as a fortysomething woman—all these things seemed to make running for political office seem like a ridiculous idea.

What Laura did, and, later, what my column did, was allow me to change the story I told about myself. In dozens of ways I had kept myself small; I'd kept my hopes and plans small. Some of this stemmed from internalizing others' ideas about me.

Working with Laura, I uncovered parts of myself I'd lost sight of. Our work together reminded me that I'd known for a long time that I had leadership qualities. I was elected president of Mrs. McMurray's first-grade class, circa 1974. I don't recall what the actual responsibilities were. Perhaps they involved guidelines for snack time or "show and share"; I'm not sure. But clearly I loved it enough that I successfully ran for student body president in both eighth and twelfth grades. Even at that age, I enjoyed thinking about policy and how to make meaningful change—even if it was just within the context of a school setting.

In my junior year of high school, I played Democratic vice presidential candidate Geraldine Ferraro in my high school's political convention. A tomboy, I was more concerned about my heels and pantyhose than my performance. But despite wrestling with my wig and enduring catcalls from some of my more chauvinistic classmates, I loved every minute of it. I was comfortable at the podium delivering my speech and cracked a few impromptu jokes. I felt so alive and "on purpose."

But I just couldn't envision running for public office as a woman who is gay and out. I knew someone had to be a trailblazer, but at that time I didn't have the confidence or the thick skin to be that person. For a long time I felt pretty disappointed in myself that I couldn't find my political voice and my courage.

Now I understand that, in addition to needing a change in societal attitudes regarding sexual orientation, I also needed to gain a different understanding of the kind of leader I wanted to be before I would run for office.

So, although I felt that deep calling back in the mid-1980s, I didn't make the decision to run for a public office until 2013—thirty years later—when I ran for Vermont State Senate. It wasn't an easy decision to make, even at that later point in my life. I've thought a lot about how I took that big step.

ALTHOUGH WE'RE ALL personally affected by thousands of small interactions and moments of revelation, I know there are four specific influences that have greatly shaped my belief that being wholehearted in our work is a key to success, and we can lead from and through this wholeheartedness.

The first major influence on my understanding of leadership was working at a place called Farm and Wilderness in central Vermont. Farm and Wilderness has seven camps in the Plymouth Valley that are rooted in Quaker philosophy and practice. In 1994, I started work there as a rock-climbing instructor and backpacking trip leader, and almost immediately sensed that I had arrived home.

I worked there for seven years and went on to direct one of their camps. The Farm and Wilderness Foundation is passionate in its conviction that we must find light—or goodness—in all people. I use this frame of reference in my work in the legislature all the time. It's easy to find goodness in the hearts of those with whom we agree. It's more challenging, but even more vital, to find this light in those with whom we disagree.

I'm not a masochist, nor am I a fool. But I'm sure that we show the best kind of leadership when we try to see beyond the words and to understand the feelings beneath the words. Why is this person feeling so angry, scared, or hurt? What can I say to help alleviate the fear or the anger? What can I offer that will bridge the gap between us?

Numerous times, I've called a constituent whom I knew disagreed with me on a particular vote. We would talk, sometimes heatedly, and invariably the person would thank me for calling—even if we still disagreed. I've come to understand that most people want to be seen for the entirety of who they are, and not just be defined by a particular issue.

For a leader, it's critical to make careful, deliberative decisions. But how we conduct ourselves in that deliberation, and in the aftermath, is just as important as the decision itself. This is where I come to the second major influence on my thinking about leadership: Dr. Brené Brown.

Brown is a professor at the University of Houston. Through her years of research, she's uncovered that there is only one way to find true connection with others—and that is to be vulnerable and show your true self. We have to let others really see us for who we truly are, and we must have faith that somehow they will respect us anyway, despite our faults.

That sounds pretty simple, but it's anything but easy. If it were easy, more folks would do it, and we wouldn't have a society in which we freely point out others' faults without being willing to examine our own. For leaders, though, it's important to acknowledge fears and mistakes and not pretend to be invincible. I don't think my readers, my constituents, or my colleagues truly want perfection; they want authenticity. But sometimes we all need to be reminded of that.

Several years ago I wrapped up an interview with a reporter, and he hung around for a few moments. I could tell he had something else he wanted to say or ask me, off the record. "Becca," he said, "I worry about you sometimes."

I was intrigued and replied, "You do?"

"Yes," he explained, "I watch you, and you bring your heart to your work, and it's really great. But I worry that this place will eat you alive. I've seen people come in with so much optimism and hope, and they just get crushed. Or they become really bitter."

I put my hand on his arm and reassured him, "You don't need to worry because I know who I am."

MY WORK WITH LAURA, described above, was the third major influence on my leadership path. The fourth and final experience that influenced my leadership philosophy provided me with the foundation I needed to have before I felt ready to run for public office. And that was to be trained as a personal coach through the Co-Active Training Institute, the program I mentioned earlier. It taught me how to ask the right questions of myself and others. It also guided me to a much deeper understanding of my own values and how to live those values.

We often talk about values in the sense of actions we take to live more politically conscious lives—conserving electricity, having a small carbon footprint, eating locally—those sorts of things. Although these are all worthy practices and ideals, these are not the values I'm talking about. I'm talking about those things in our lives and spirits that we value the most. Not possessions. Not simply actions. But *experiences*. And a way of being in the world.

My list includes: authenticity, empathy, justice, vulnerability, connection, hope, and taking action to make positive change. These are the things that both move me and fulfill me. I regularly ask myself: How am I honoring these values? How am I living these values that are so important to me?

The spirit of our work matters. Our daily interactions with others matter. Intentionally living our values cannot be an afterthought—it must be a central part of our work. Our leadership comes from within and is shown to others not just in times of crisis and uncertainty but day in and day out in the way we treat colleagues and neighbors.

It's not very difficult to find leadership qualities in those around you. In small ways every day, members of our teams and colleagues at our organizations are doing good work. We all need to remember to recognize and acknowledge the good work of those around us.

Initially, I was trained as a coach to do this with my clients, to help them see their gifts, but now it's simply a part of my daily habits. When I see good work, I try to name it and acknowledge it directly to the person accomplishing it. And then I champion it to others when I have the opportunity.

We all want to be seen. We want our contributions to be noticed. Not because we need credit, but because we want a basic kind of acknowledgment that we're here and we matter. And good leadership requires allies; it's not practiced in isolation. All these small interactions help us construct a network of people who know that we truly value each other.

As you read this collection, remember that it is also a curation, although I hope it does not shy away from showing you who I am as a person, warts and all. I want to share what I care about, how I think, and how I live my values. The following pieces are organized loosely around those values: authenticity, justice, connection, hope, taking action to make positive change, and, of course, hard-earned vulnerability— straight from the girl in the yellow pantsuit who has taught her grown-up self that being audacious, daring, and vulnerable is an essential part of inviting others to create a vision of a better world that works for all of us and to join the effort to build it.

Part One

❧

Authenticity

Picturing Yourself

§

A T THE END of a speech I gave to the Girls' State program several years ago, one of the high school students asked me about my political heroes. The students were clearly surprised when I named my political icons. They weren't politicians they'd ever heard of before: Bella Abzug, Geraldine Ferraro, Barbara Jordan, Tammy Baldwin, and my greatest political hero, Shirley Chisholm— the first Black woman elected to Congress. These women, trailblazers all, were the ones who had helped me imagine a political life for myself when I personally knew no one in politics and couldn't quite visualize a path I could follow.

I never get tired of watching old video footage of Shirley Chisholm's speeches. The seven-term congresswoman some-how managed to be simultaneously matter of fact and inspiring. Born in Brooklyn to a mother from Barbados and a father from Guyana, she spent chunks of her childhood in Barbados with her grandmother. Her mother was a domestic worker; her father worked in a factory. As a working-class

Black woman, and as the child of immigrants, Chisholm constantly—and skillfully—navigated a political world in which she was not supposed to succeed.

Yet she deeply understood her strengths and skills. She once said, "My greatest political asset, which professional politicians fear, is my mouth, out of which come all kinds of things one shouldn't always discuss for reasons of political expediency." And she exuded a beautiful confidence. I still marvel at her self-possession.

When Chisholm announced her historic run for president, she had few political role models to turn to, and yet she still unabashedly owned the stage. When I feel down about my work in Montpelier, I watch video clips of Chisholm. Her self-assurance always centers and inspires me.

I'm no Shirley Chisholm, but I know I'm in a unique position to help guide young people who want to find a place for themselves in politics. Recently I became involved in a program called Girls Rock the Capitol (GRTC) run by the Girl Scouts of the Green and White Mountains. GRTC is a legislative internship and mentoring program for high school girls that pairs students with female legislators. I'm excited to participate—and also a little sad for my teenage self, that I'd not had a similar program.

My mentee is a teen I've known since she was a baby when her parents and I worked together at Farm & Wilderness in Plymouth, Vermont. She participated in the legislative page program at the Vermont Statehouse when she was in eighth grade, and that special experience got her curious about a life in politics.

After our first of several "shadowing" days, I asked her to reflect upon and write about her initial impressions. She said astutely, "Power is held mostly in the personal relationships and connections that are made, and the vitality of these connections." She also remarked on how fascinating it is to watch the interactions of people who are politically or philosophically pitted against each other but must still work together. Even legislators who are ostensibly in opposition to each other must build strong daily relationships. My young mentee ended her reflection with the realization that diplomacy was critically important—even in our small state.

She closed by expressing her sincerest gratitude that she has the opportunity to see the legislature in action though my willingness to mentor her. But I think I felt even more thankful for the chance to use my position to stretch her understanding of the political world and to help her see that she can have a place in it.

Celebrating Successes

§

RECENTLY I took my ebullient labradoodle on a run through woods and fields. At one point my dog caught the scent of something divine; he was off and running, with his nose pushed up against the field's stubble. I assumed it was the smell of a mole or shrew that was demanding his attention. I stood, transfixed, watching his dogged search. He then bounded up and crested a hill, and a wild cacophony of honks and bleats filled the air. A great mass of geese—I estimated around 150 birds—took flight at once. He then turned back to look at me as if to say, proudly, "Look! Look what I did!"

Unlike my dog, most of us don't take the time to celebrate our successes. We especially don't take note of the relatively minor ones that mark our day-to-day lives. We tend to focus on all the things we haven't completed—and let's be honest—the ones we haven't even started yet. Like most of my friends, I have a list of chores and projects I'd like to get done. As I write this, my firewood needs stacking, my brush needs trimming, and I have yet to put away my summer patio furniture.

Turning to the interior of my home, there's an additional list of shortcomings to be noted and catalogued. The truth is, the lists will keep growing evermore, and haunt me like an Edgar Allan Poe refrain. As soon as I've crossed something off, another millstone is added. What's to be done about such a maddening, unsatisfactory cycle? I've started making a point of celebrating minor successes—the small but lovely bits that truly make up the bulk of our lives.

A minor success that still delights me is that I finally managed to get my seven-year-old daughter to walk from the car into the school and to her classroom without me. This morning, after my concerted encouragement, she allowed her big brother to walk her into the school.

When she agreed to this arrangement, she made sure that she articulated her parameters: "Just so you know, I will only do this on 'All-School Sing' days because I know I'll see you soon." Her stipulation thus voiced, she happily scampered into the building. I did a little victory cheer in the car as I watched them go.

Later that morning, to reinforce and honor my feelings I told a friend about what had happened. She exclaimed, "That's huge!" It was not said at all ironically; she knew this was an important milestone for both my daughter and for me. The act of telling someone else helped to solidify my feeling of accomplishment.

I've also realized recently how critical it is to take the time to acknowledge when I've taken a risk—even if I'm the only one who truly understands the bravery I've employed.

I made a decision a few weeks ago to approach my public work with a different kind of openness. A friend helped me realize I had a "stage voice" and an "everyday voice"; I thought about what would happen if I blended these more seamlessly and openly. I wasn't sure what it would feel like or whether it would have the desired impact on my audience. It felt both intriguing and risky.

I've now given several speeches with this frame in mind. And after each one, I celebrated the realization of my goal but also the deeper impact I had on my audience. I sensed a new, deeper level of connection with others and also, surprisingly, with myself. Perhaps the change was only truly palpable to me. No matter. I felt like my dog: "Look! Look what I did!"

From Bondswoman
to Best-Selling Author

§

NOVEMBER 18, 2014

I N 2001, Harvard University professor Henry Louis Gates
Jr. purchased a remarkable novel—purportedly written by
an African American woman who'd escaped slavery—at
auction.

Gates attended the annual auction by the Swann Galleries
in New York City, which offers artifacts and memorabilia of
African American history, and paid about $8,000 for a 300-
page manuscript, believed to be the first novel penned by
an African American woman. The unpublished book—*The
Bondswoman's Narrative: A Novel by Hannah Crafts*—had
spent decades languishing in an attic in New Jersey before
historian and bibliographer Dorothy Porter Wesley bought
it. After Wesley's death, the literary treasure found its way
to Gates, who had the book scientifically authenticated as
having been written sometime in the late 1850s. He edited
and published the book in 2002, and it immediately became

a best seller. But the mystery remained: Who was Hannah Crafts?

Winthrop University English professor Gregg Hecimovich reconstructed the life story of this remarkable African American woman.[1*] He spent nearly a decade combing through primary-source documents to positively identify Hannah Crafts as an escaped slave named Hannah Bond. As a trained historian myself, I have spent hundreds of hours relishing old documents. I got chills when it was announced that Hecimovich will publish a book next year that reconstructs the life of this intriguing woman: *The Life and Times of Hannah Crafts.*

Hollis Robbins, chair of the humanities department of the Peabody Institute and director of Africana Studies at Johns Hopkins, together with Gates, set out to trace the author's literary influences, which included the works of Charlotte Brontë, Walter Scott, William Shakespeare, Charles Dickens, and many other literary giants. Robins and Gates concluded that Bond must have been an enslaved housemaid in the residence of John H. Wheeler of Murfreesboro, North Carolina. She'd left a riveting clue in her text: the master in her book serves as the United States minister (ambassador) to Nicaragua. Wheeler did just that, and his library included all the literature that Bond references in her writing—except one: Dickens' *Bleak House.* How had Hannah Bond learned passages of *Bleak House* if it was not in Wheeler's library?

Hecimovich's detective work reveals that girls from a nearby school boarded with the Wheeler family, and their school's curriculum required them to read and memorize passages of the Dickens novel. Hecimovich's plausible

---

[1*] Professor Hecimovich now teaches at Furman University.

explanation is that Bond either heard the girls' recitations of passages or borrowed a copy from one of the girls, with or without consent.

The forthcoming book will reconstruct the lives of seven enslaved individuals in the Wheeler household who had both the means and the opportunity to write the manuscript. Hecimovich sets his detective work against the rich cultural background of mixed-race society in the decade leading up to the Civil War. I can't remember when I've been so excited about a book release. This book will be a welcome antidote to the scourge of racism that emboldens citizens to disparage and discount our first African American president.

Hecimovich explains the powerful impact his research will have, not only because of its relevance to African American history and the literary canon, but also because it tells us so much about ourselves as a nation. "Crafts' life," he writes, "endures through her art, a voice rediscovered, unmasking and challenging the racial bigotry and greed that divide people and nations—then and now." He aptly concludes that "literature can still transcend the divisions of race, gender, class, and time to imagine and substantiate justice and freedom."

Grandma's Kung Fu Fighting

§

OCTOBER 2, 2012

MY MOM WAS NOT ALWAYS a kung fu black belt. Like many women of her generation, she worked extremely hard raising children and managing our home. Twice she lived overseas—in Germany and in Switzerland—because of my father's job. When we were out of elementary school, my mom fixed timepieces in a watch factory and then slogged away at an insurance company call center. She discovered her true calling—after we all left for college—when she took up tai chi to help her aching back. My mom did not know then that these first tentative steps were the beginning of a career. Now my parents' home is full of medals and trophies won, certificates earned, and weapons that my mom wields. Dad has adjusted to carrying her cache of swords, staffs, fighting fans, and other assorted bludgeons, but Mom's not quite accustomed to the accolades she receives as a well-respected martial arts instructor. From *hausfrau* to crouching tiger: she reinvented herself.

We constantly allow—encourage, even—politicians, celebrities, and all too many televangelists to reinvent themselves, but we rarely give ourselves the same permission. We imagine our own identities as fixed and immutable. In this light, I recently reconsidered a conversation I had with a friend last year. While discussing her house renovations, I asked if she had taken any before-and-after pictures of the work they'd done. She replied quickly and decisively, "Oh, no. We're not those kinds of people." I was dumbstruck: what does snapping a few home remodeling pictures say about a person? And why is she so adamant that her family are not "those kinds" of people?

We regularly and unconsciously define ourselves against an imagined Other and then use this comparison to create a sense of ourselves. Based on our memories and the stories we tell about ourselves, these notions are just that—ideas. We make these stories The Story of our lives. And The Story—if we let it define us—limits us, reducing the choices we imagine for ourselves.

Ulric Neisser, an influential psychological researcher, challenged our long-held beliefs about the accuracy of our remembered stories. Neisser died in February, and Douglas Martin of the *New York Times* remembered him as a scientist who "helped lead a postwar revolution in the study of the human mind" through his research on perception and memory. He resisted the dominant post–World War II psychology discipline, behaviorism, and in the process created a new field—cognitive psychology. As Martin explains, Neisser's research showed that "memory is a reconstruction of the past, not an accurate snapshot of it." People think they remember actual events in near-perfect detail when they actually remember memories—and in some instances, they remember memories of memories. Not great stuff upon which to build a static identity.

Years ago an acquaintance of mine wanted to quit smoking, but, in addition to the addiction itself, she simply couldn't get beyond the fact that she defined herself as A Smoker. When she saw joggers zip past her house, she mocked them, inwardly or with her friends. She never imagined that she could be that runner she was so busy ridiculing; that simply didn't fit her self-concept. Then it occurred to her that this was just a story she told about herself, and she could actually tell a different story. Over time she altered her ideas about herself and tried out another identity: Runner.

It is difficult to change the story if your friends discourage it. Nicholas Christakis, a social scientist and internist at Harvard, and James Fowler, a political scientist at UC San Diego, document this difficulty in their groundbreaking social-network mapping of the famous Framingham Heart Study (FHS). This research—originally started in Framingham, Massachusetts, in 1948 with more than 5,000 subjects—is a cardiovascular study that now spans three generations. Christakis and Fowler mapped the social networks of the original FHS participants and discovered that obesity, smoking, and even happiness appear to be passed among friends and families just like viruses.

There is strong evidence that the 12,630 individuals in the FHS social network spread obesity person-to-person. If your friends or family members became obese, you were much more likely to become obese yourself. Christakis and Fowler theorize that obesity becomes normalized among cohorts, and this shifting view of obesity makes it much more permissible to gain weight. Similar patterns emerged when they tracked smoking rates among the FHS social network. Says Fowler, "People quit together, or they didn't quit at all." He and Christakis even observed that happy people tend to hang out with happy people and spread happiness within their social networks.

Napoleon Hill, writer and advisor to presidents Woodrow Wilson and Franklin Roosevelt, asserted, "What the mind of man can conceive and believe, it can achieve." His book *Think and Grow Rich* (1939) is one of the best-selling books of all time and still, seventy-five years after it first appeared, makes "Top 10" lists of business books. Hill identified something that many of us know but find difficult to put into practice: our ideas absolutely help shape who we become, and we can change these ideas to become who we want to be. So don't dump your friends or cut yourself off from that cousin who constantly berates you about your weight or your housekeeping. But do surround yourself with people who believe that transformation is possible.

My mom's facing major surgery this year; she may have to stop her kung fu fighting. As painful as this will be for her, we in her network will encourage her to transform once again. I can't wait to see what comes next.

My Little Collector

§

ACH MORNING I sidestep miniature pirate accoutrements strewn across the floor and gather my kids' coats and backpacks. As I reach for the doorknob, my son gives me a desperate look and cries, "We forgot my Playmobil magazine!" I dutifully swallow my stock speech about how "we" is not really appropriate here. Instead, I prompt him to look in all the usual spots. He locates his much-cherished catalogue and stuffs the dog-eared guide into his backpack. Around this time I start to feel like Bill Murray in *Groundhog Day*—reliving the same banal scenario over and over again with no inkling that a scintilla of change has occurred. Like that hapless weatherman stuck in the wretched time loop, I search for meaning in this absurd routine.

My son is a Playmobil collector—one might say "aficionado." And like any collector, he studies his compilation constantly. Although many parents might push their offspring towards a collection with more gravitas and substance, say, stamps or currency, kids choose their own collecting obsessions. I guess I should be grateful he hasn't latched on to Pokémon cards or a collection of animal scat.

A friend joked recently that Playmobil designers hate parents. Considering the infinitesimal pirate treasure that gets scattered absolutely everywhere, the miniscule "snap-on" cuffs for the soldiers, and tiny flip-flops for Playmobil beachgoers, she has a point. More than once I've called out "Curse you, Playmobil!" while cleaning the house. A pal coached me to just suck up the Playmobil accessories with my vacuum sans guilt, but I know that would bring more heartache. You see, like any avid collector, my son knows exactly which swords fit with which pirate set, which treasure chest goes with which boat, and he will assuredly enlist my assistance to search for anything missing. And search. And search. If the piece in question is actually in the vacuum, I am doomed to a life of eternal searching.

Once we looked for a Viking's plastic hair for days. It had popped off and rolled behind the file cabinet. Despite my urgings that we substitute hair from one of the other Viking figures, my son reminded me that the hair in question was orange. He couldn't possibly make the Viking a towhead or a brunette. It's not that he isn't willing to mix and match his accessories; he just knew that he had only a few redheads in his collection; he wasn't going to let it go that easily.

Hans Beck, a cabinetmaker and model airplane designer, certainly knew what he was doing when he invented the Playmobil figures in 1971. At first, German toymakers were uninterested. But that changed with the worldwide oil crisis of 1973–74, as toymakers sought to develop toys that required less plastic. Beck's play figures are now ubiquitous around the world.

As Beck explained to the *Christian Science Monitor* in 1997, "My figures were quite simple, but they allowed children room for their imagination." Those nearly three-inch-tall figures—first referred to as "klickies"—haven't really changed over the years: the heads, arms, legs, and hands still move, and the figures still have benign smiles and no noses. Andrea Schauer, CEO of the Brandstätter Group, manufacturer of Playmobil, said in a recent interview that although the figures haven't changed much in four decades, Playmobil takes children's feedback very seriously: "After all, children are the ones who have to like our products." She asserts that although their sets still allow for great imaginative play, "Playmobil play worlds have become more sophisticated and diverse."

Occasionally—despite having sold more than 2.6 billion figures—Playmobil misses the mark. There was that nineteenth-century Chinese railroad-worker "coolie" display that customers judged to be in poor taste. And then there was a set featuring medieval punishments: public stocks for smiley criminals and a "baker's cage" for dunking in the river those tiny bakers whose loaves are deemed substandard. Beck insists that you must show all sides of history, distasteful or not.

I can think of more than a few important exceptions to this assertion, but I have to admit my six-year-old son has already learned a tremendous amount about history from his Playmobil sets. We've had rich, detailed conversations about the era of the Caribbean pirates, types of Roman weaponry, and the woolly mammoths of the Ice Age.

He even loves to crack jokes about his Playmobil figures: "Mom, you know why these Playmobil people couldn't have made those cave drawings and handprints? They can't open their fingers!" He then demonstrates what it would look like for figures with hands curved in a permanent "C" to make artwork. It's funny. Every time.

Mark McKinley, writing in the *National Psychologist*, lists the many reasons why humans collect things: for fun and enjoyment, connecting with others who share similar interests, and viewing collecting as a big quest. Still others derive pleasure from "experimenting with arranging, rearranging, and classifying parts of a-big-world-out-there." According to McKinley, collecting can also serve as a means of control to elicit a comfort zone in one's life—a way to calm fears and ease insecurity.

Knowing that there are important social and psychological reasons behind this Playmobil obsession soothes my anxiety and eases my insecurity as we monitor his desire for set after set. When he says he wants all the Playmobils in the world, he's not kidding. We feel unsupportive of his obsession when we joke that we will not drain his as yet meagre college fund to support his collecting habit. But unlike in the time warp of *Groundhog Day*, there's always a fresh new day—complete with new Playmobils—and we are assuredly going to make a few more trips to the toy store.

Taking Ego Out of It

§

T O MAINTAIN MY ENERGY and focus during the legislative session, I bundle up and head out each morning into Hubbard Park, the lovely woodland behind the statehouse. On a run in the park last week with a small white labradoodle (mine) and a large black goldendoodle (my roomie's), I watched the dogs jockey and angle for the position of "top dog" on the trail. I thought about ego and how it can often get in the way.

I've been ruminating on the aspects of human nature that can prevent us from doing our best work, both individually and collectively. Ego itself can certainly be an impediment to smooth and effective process. The more we value our individual part of any undertaking over the collaborative process itself, the more we can develop an outsized sense of our own importance. And our attachment to the "ownership" of ideas may stop us from accepting and celebrating collective achievement.

This obviously plays out, to some extent, in all workplaces. In the statehouse, it can take the form of legislators sometimes feeling possessive about a particular area of the law. It is not unusual to hear someone say something to the effect of: "I usually do the bills on that. Why did she put in that bill? That's my area." Or individual legislators will take credit for a particular piece of legislation even though it takes many, many contributors to bring any bill through the long, complicated process of becoming a law.

Elizabeth Gilbert—author of *Eat, Pray, Love*—gave a TED Talk in 2009 that helped me to shape my own understanding of creativity, genius, and the "ownership" of ideas. Gilbert's talk references the ancient Greeks and Romans and their ideas about divine intervention and creativity. She says of the classical age, "People believed that creativity was this divine attendant spirit that came to human beings from some distant and unknowable source, for distant and unknowable reasons." The Greeks referred to these spirits of creativity as *daemons*. Similarly, Gilbert explains, the Romans called a "disembodied creative spirit a *genius*." And *genius* did not refer to a very creative or clever individual. Instead, a genius was a magical entity or divine spirit that would "invisibly assist the artist with their work and would shape the outcome of that work."

Significant comfort and relief can be found in viewing oneself as a conduit for ideas—and not the creator. As Gilbert points out, the artist or writer is then protected from an inflated ego or narcissism. She explains that if your work is brilliant, you can't take all the credit for it because everybody understands that you had a "disembodied genius who had helped you." And, conversely, if your final product is awful, you can blame that, in part, on your daemon or genius. Gilbert identifies the Renaissance and Enlightenment as the culprits for the shift away from this liberating ideal and towards a more constricted, constructed view of creativity—one that puts individuals in the center of the equation. This changing conception of genius reached its zenith in the Romantic notion of the tortured genius, and many of us still think of the anguished musician or writer toiling away in solitude. She bemoans the fact that now "there's no more room for mystical creatures who take dictation from the divine." This is a big loss for all of us.

In my years of writing this column, there have been times when I've had to work mightily to pull my thoughts into some semblance of coherence. Yet, at other times, whole paragraphs truly seem to come to me from beyond, and the column writes itself. I can't anticipate when this will happen, but the trick I've found is to imagine that my ideas are not wholly mine; they are just passing through.

The Liberace of the Ring

§

DECEMBER 4, 2012

AS UNLIKELY AS IT SOUNDS, I not only knew who boxer Hector "Macho" Camacho was, when his death was announced last week, but I was also saddened by the news. Camacho, age fifty, was considered by many to be one of the most talented boxers of his generation. As Matt Schudel of the *Washington Post* noted, Camacho combined "charisma and color" with lightning speed, earning him the nickname "Rambo-Liberace" from HBO boxing analyst Larry Merchant. Merchant maintained that the fans adored Camacho because he was equal parts "He-Man and showman."

Camacho—who died as a result of a gunshot wound to the head—was killed in the same town in which he was born, Bayamon, Puerto Rico, but his ascent to greatness began on the streets of Spanish Harlem in New York City. A self-described street fighter, Camacho said in 1982, after dispatching Johnny Sato in just four rounds and earning $50,000 for the drubbing:

23

"A few years ago, if I had met Sato on 115th Street, I would have done the same thing for nothing."

An undeniably scrappy, wisecracking pugilist, Camacho also had an outrageously flamboyant side that seemed incongruous with his gritty, street-smart life. Take a moment to search for Camacho photos on the Web. You'll find gladiator outfits, sequined loincloths, black fox-fur robes—and always that boyish spit curl over his forehead. He loved a good show, and he had the exquisite talent and instinct to deliver.

A world champion in three different weight classes, Camacho demonstrated his boxing skills early. As Bruce Weber of the *New York Times* recalled, boxing legend Sugar Ray Leonard recognized—when Camacho was only twenty years old—that the rookie fighter would eventually be coming for him. "I told him that people are always asking who's going to take my place," Leonard recalled. "I told him he could." What set Camacho apart was that, despite being a boxer, he was never a slugger. Instead, he combined superb agility, intricate footwork, and high-speed precise punches to stun his opponents and amaze spectators.

So how did I come to know about Hector "Macho" Camacho, Ray "Boom-Boom" Mancini, Oscar De La Hoya, and other boxing stars? From a most unlikely source: Alyson, one of my best friends in high school, was an avid boxing fan. Although I don't recall her having the DJ play Camacho's signature theme song, "Macho Man," at her Bat Mitzvah, it's quite possible she did. Diminutive and not at all brash, Alyson had a love for boxing that was both huge and fierce. She brought her boxing magazines to school and kept us all up to date on significant boxing stats and important upcoming matches. A member of the Future Business Leaders of America, she was determined to have a career which combined her prodigious writing skills and her love of sports. Now, decades later, I can happily report that she has been one of Michael Jordan's most trusted PR writers for many years. If she ever felt self-conscious about her unconventional interest in the boxing world, she never let on. It was simply an extension of an inner confidence that is hard to find at forty-four—let alone at sixteen.

When we all bemoaned Coke's ill-conceived plan to change its formula, it made no difference to her; she'd always enjoyed a Pepsi with her lunch. When my friends and I took the drama club by storm, Alyson embraced her own niche at our high school theater—running the box office. Her organization skills were second to none, but more important than her financial acumen or her impeccable orderliness, she exuded a love for making the spectacles "go."

Today she is still a savvy, whip-smart fan who does not merely cheer from the side lines but puts her skills to work for the good of the show.

Alyson also deeply appreciates "the fight" in others. Her mighty love for her father—and her great admiration for his courage in battling kidney disease—was tremendously tender. He was her lifelong touchstone and best friend, and she saw and revered his greatness each day. Which is not to say that she remembers him as perfect or uncomplicated; she's too grounded and pragmatic for that. She holds the memory of his humanity and imperfection while also acknowledging the many ways in which he touched the edge of magnificence. This is the same inimitable quality that enabled her to embrace the often seedy and messy world of boxing while being impeccably "put together" herself.

Bits of Camacho's unsavory, troubled personal life followed him even in death. Mourners at his wake and funeral this week had a ringside seat for bare-knuckle fisticuffs between several of his ex-girlfriends and his sisters. But this unseemly media circus is not what holds my interest. It's his broad, boyish grin that said, "Love me. Love all of me—even the shady parts."

Laura Hillenbrand, award-winning nonfiction author of *Seabiscuit: An American Legend,* once said about jockey Red Pollard, one of her book's heroes, "He wasn't a great jockey, but the moments he was on Seabiscuit, he was great." Similarly, Hector "Macho" Camacho showed the depth of his talent best when he was in the ring.

I will never be an avid boxing fan like my buddy, but having her in my circle of friends reminds me that we must find flashes of greatness wherever we can, while accepting that greatness comes in ragged packages. Stubbornly human as we are, what more can we ask for?

"Tween" Mean

§

FEBRUARY 4, 2014

A FRIEND'S DAUGHTER struggles to navigate a school landscape filled with "mean girls." The social scene seems nearly impossible to traverse safely; a devastating look or a barely audible comment is awfully hard for a teacher to notice—let alone regulate. I know this because, for several years, I was one of the mean girls.

I didn't start out as a bully. I was well liked in fifth grade, and—despite being chubby—easily made friends. But then we moved. I was tossed in among group of kids who referred to me as a "heavy hitter." A talented softball player, I was too chunky to simply be admired for my skill. Compliments came nestled in put-downs. I felt ambushed; I'd never before been teased at school because of my weight.

And then, in sixth grade, someone scrawled "lezzie" on my locker, and I could feel myself being swept out to sea.

To survive the tide of cruelty, I sought a lifebuoy. Everything feels desperate at twelve. I stayed afloat by falling in with a group of "cool" (read: mean) girls. They appreciated my wicked humor, and I used my wisecracks as a "tribute" payment. As long as I made them laugh, I was not their target. I was not mature or self-confident enough to use victimless humor, so I sometimes said devastatingly mean things; I couldn't let myself be banished permanently to the bottom rung of the social ladder.

A girl in our class told a teacher that I, along with my "clique," had teased her on the bus, and the teacher confronted me. It was true, undeniably. But I felt betrayed by this teacher. Where was she when I'd been the butt of the jokes? She jumped into the discussion midstream and now expected me to trust her. I didn't feel safe sharing with her that I'd also been tormented. As we are all prone to do, she drew a fairly tidy map of the bullies and the bullied. But I knew even then that tweens often change positions, frantically scrambling for a foothold.

Although our attention usually focuses on high school students who are bullied, a UCLA study revealed that almost half of middle school students who were surveyed reported being bullied during a one-week period. Jaana Juvonen—UCLA professor of psychology and co-author of the study—notes, "Bullying is a problem that large numbers of kids confront. . . . It's not just an issue for a few unfortunate ones." She was surprised that so many students experienced bullying within such a short time—just five days. A study from the Oregon Research Institute published in the *Journal of Early Adolescence* found similar results: roughly four out of five middle school students reported being verbally harassed at school.

In the UCLA study, bullying included name calling,

spreading rumors, or kicking and shoving in hallways. Verbal harassment occurred twice as often as physical aggression, and it cut across all income brackets and ethnic backgrounds. Interestingly, the old adage about "sticks and stones" does not hold true. Students who were physically bullied and those who were verbally bullied felt the same levels of anxiety and fear: Juvonen found that all kids who had been bullied in some way reported feeling humiliated or anxious, or disliking school.

A study conducted by the Institute of Education in London revealed that less than 1 percent of elementary students could be characterized as "true bullies"—those who bully and are not bullied themselves. More frequently, the very same students who are sometimes the victims are also sometimes the perpetrators. Dr. Leslie Gutman, lead researcher, explained, "We are not suggesting that schools adopt a soft approach to bullying but simply stating that, on the basis of evidence, bullying is more complex an issue than some people believe it to be." We must focus on bullying behavior in all its forms. This is much more honest and useful than simply labeling students as either "victims" or "bullies"—especially given that bullying behavior extends to adults as well.

There have been several high-profile national cases of principals who bullied parents and teachers, as well as infamous examples of teachers bullying other teachers or students. Studies from the Workplace Bullying Institute (WBI) indicate that the professionals most likely to be bullying targets are schoolteachers and school nurses. Dr. Gary Namie, writing in the WBI's 2013 industry survey, reflected on our national effort to curb student bullying: "How in the world can youngsters ever be persuaded to stop when they witness adult bullying in the schools?"

I am always incredulous and disheartened when a friend or colleague says, "Well, she's never bullied me." Or: "But he's so good at _____" (fill in any particular skill here)—implying that, because this supervisor has other valuable skills, he couldn't possibly bully others. Just like those surreptitious mean "tween" whisperings, bullying is not always obvious.

We must ask ourselves: Do the stated values of a school match the reality on the ground? Kids notice everything. Is the entire school staff striving for indisputable, unwavering kindness and respect? And are our educators truly tuned in to the students' delicate and ever-changing social dance? The position of victims and bullies is rarely static, but the behavior is always abhorrent.

Some of the girls I bullied in middle school are now among my very best friends. And one of my proudest moments in twelfth grade was being voted "most humorous" by my classmates. For, although I'd earned the same honor in eighth grade, by the time I graduated from high school I had figured out how to be funny without being mean. I wish there had been a vibrant social curriculum in place to help me learn that sooner.

Building Character

§

NOVEMBER 5, 2013

"JUST BE AWARE that there's been a bear sighted in and around the campsites." I sent Jedi mind-control messages to the park employee: *Stop talking!* But too late—my kids had already engaged their bionic ears. My loquacious three-year-old called from the back seat, "Oh, good! I hope we'll see a bear. I'd really like to see a bear. Do you think we'll see a bear?" Her equally chatty five-year-old brother shouted over her, "Bear? Oh no! I don't want to see a bear. I really don't want to see a bear. Do you think we'll see a bear?" Thus began our very first family camping trip.

I want my children to feel comfortable and capable in the woods. Leading adolescents on backpacking trips throughout the Northeast gave me tremendous self-knowledge and cemented in me a generally irrepressible faith that I can get out of just about any jam. I want my kids to feel that same confidence and ease—both in nature and in facing life's persistent flow of adversity and triumph.

But as we set up our tent amid the constant din of worry and expectation about the resident bear, doubt skulked in: *Why, exactly, did we think this would be fun?* Friedrich Nietzsche came to mind: "To live is to suffer, to survive is to find some meaning in the suffering." But instead of referencing the wildly chipper Nietzsche, I should have called upon Dr. Martin Seligman for guidance and comfort.

Seligman—author and highly esteemed psychology professor at the University of Pennsylvania—has written extensively on the topics of learned helplessness and positive psychology. His books include *Learned Optimism, Authentic Happiness, and Flourish.* Seligman (sometimes referred to as "the Happiness Doctor") critically evaluated the latest edition of the *Diagnostic and Statistical Manual of Mental Disorders* (DSM-V) and offered a positive alternative—*Character Strengths and Virtues: A Handbook and Classification* (CSV), co-authored with the late Christopher Peterson, an award-winning professor of psychology at the University of Michigan.

The CSV was the first attempt by the psychology research community to identify and classify human beings' positive psychological traits. It names six core virtues that the authors assert are almost universally considered good in societies throughout history: Wisdom and Knowledge, Courage, Humanity, Justice, Temperance, and Transcendence. For each valued trait, Seligman and Peterson enumerate associated character strengths: creativity, curiosity, open-mindedness, love of learning, etc.

In "What If the Secret to Success Is Failure?"—a fascinating investigation of how two very different schools have employed aspects of the CSV—*New York Times* contributing writer Paul

Tough highlights two innovative school leaders: Dominic Randolph at the exceedingly exclusive Riverdale Country School (the yearly tuition, excluding fees and supplies, is $37,000), and David Levin, cofounder of the free KIPP Network of charter schools in educationally underserved communities. Riverdale serves an overwhelmingly White, affluent population, while KIPP focuses on increasing the academic performance of predominantly Black and Latino students from low-income families. Yet, despite their different school populations, both Randolph and Levin see test scores as poor predictors of lifelong success.

They separately concluded that the kids who succeeded both in school and beyond were not the ones with the highest test scores or the highest IQs but the ones that possessed "grit." Intrigued, they turned to Seligman's work to help them nurture something in their students that is both critical and elusive: character.

Randolph describes why he was drawn to emphasize Seligman's CSV as an alternative to an emphasis on standardized testing: "This push on tests is missing out on some serious parts of what it means to be a successful human." Randolph worries that his privileged and protected students have no idea how to face real adversity. And Levin, whose students face acute hardship every day, is troubled by the number of students who successfully complete high school but then drop out of college: "We thought, *Okay, our first class was the fifth-highest-performing class in all of New York City . . . It's all going to be solved.* But it wasn't."

With the help of Seligman and his then graduate assistant, Angela Duckworth (who recently was awarded a MacArthur "genius" fellowship), Randolph and Levin narrowed the CSV's full set of twenty-four character traits down to a more manageable handful: zest, grit, self-control, social intelligence, gratitude, optimism, and curiosity. According to Seligman's research, these qualities are especially likely to predict high achievement and life satisfaction. Both educators focused on building these character traits within their school communities because, as Tough explains, they believe that the ultimate product of good character is "a happy, meaningful, productive life." And, sometimes, to build strong character we must struggle or fail first.

It is still unclear whether schools can successfully instill in students the importance of strong character. At the very least, they can reinforce family-held values of character. What's certain, however, is that chasing after higher test scores—without acknowledging the importance of strong character—will give students (and parents) short-term feelings of accomplishment but will not equip students for genuine lifelong learning and contentment.

At 3:00 a.m., when my kids were still chattering about bears, the stars, and distant rustlings in the woods, and I was nursing a split lip from my daughter's nighttime flailing and felt a chest cold settling in, our camping trip seemed like an utter failure. At dawn, I slithered out of my bedroll—never again to be referred to as a "sleeping" bag—and fired up the nifty little backpacking stove to make coffee. I was reflecting on the shortcomings of our adventure when light rain further dampened my fortitude.

But as the coffee came to a boil, my children greeted the day with unexpected exuberance and giddiness: They had survived the night! Armed with an undeniable sense of accomplishment and a newfound bravery, they both asked the same question: When can we go camping again?

Meditating Over the Wood Pile

§

AUGUST 12, 2014

I KNOW I SHOULD MEDITATE MORE. My life is busy—harried sometimes—and quieting my mind would be a great idea. In a town like Brattleboro, I am reminded of my meditation shortcomings all the time. I can sign up for Mindful Parenting workshops, every imagined style of yoga, breath work, and Buddhist meditation. I make promise after promise: I will meditate for five minutes at the beginning and end of each day, sitting on the floor with a candle. Okay, instead: I will meditate for two minutes each morning and evening while resting on the couch. And then, finally: I will pour myself a cup of good strong coffee at dawn and think about how darn good it is. Success!

New England singer-songwriter Cheryl Wheeler has a song that captures the way many of us feel when we make these promises and don't follow through. "I should learn how to meditate and sew and bake and dance and paint and sail and make gazpacho," she sings. "I should turn my attention to repairing all those forty-year-old socks there in that bureau." After a huge litany of all the things she "should" do, including chanting "in impossible positions till my legs appear to not have any bones," Wheeler finishes with an exasperated, "I'm unworthy!"

I have felt like that, certainly, and still do in moments of despair, but a friend at Brattlemasters (our town's Toastmasters meeting) turned me on to the work of positive psychology researcher Mihály Csíkszentmihályi (pronounced Me-HIGH-ee Chick-sent-me-HIGH-ee) and his book *Flow: The Psychology of Optimal Experience.* I may still be unworthy, but now I don't feel so bad about that.

Csíkszentmihályi, a Hungarian American professor of psychology at Claremont Graduate University, asserts that "flow" is a mental state that occurs when a person is fully immersed in a task or activity. Sometimes when I'm writing I pause and find I have written four paragraphs and yet have no memory of it; the words seem to have found me. Flow is that mental "zone" you enter when you are completely absorbed in a particular task and feel contentment, even elation, from the process.

Csíkszentmihályi's interest in "flow" began when he pondered the state of complete absorption that artists sometimes experience: "getting lost" in their work. Contemporary accounts suggest that Renaissance artist Michelangelo became so engrossed in his work on his masterpiece, the Sistine Chapel, that he often went for days without meeting his basic needs. Despite lying on his back in an uncomfortable position on scaffolding, he was tremendously productive and creative. Csíkszentmihályi suspects that Michelangelo experienced flow, and this may have contributed to the artist's prodigious productivity.

In a February 2014 *Psychology Today* article, "Flow States and Creativity," author Steven Kotler highlights research indicating that the positive effects of flow are felt even after the flow state is over. Theresa Amabile, a professor at the Harvard Business School, has documented that people experience greater creativity the day after they've been in a flow state.

There may even be biological reasons for this. During a flow state, the dorsolateral prefrontal cortex—that part of the brain that monitors impulse control and works as an inner critic—goes into radio silence. When this area is deactivated, we lose self-doubt and gain more courage. Kotler asserts that this augments "our ability to imagine new possibilities and share those possibilities with the world."

I am relieved that I can gain a feeling of calm and confidence by entering a flow state, because it feels like there's little time to meditate when the three cords of firewood heaped in my backyard demand stacking. As the logs rest yet another day in their haphazard repose, I know their little bark jackets molder as they start their slouch towards decay. And I imagine the grass beneath gasping for breath as the sun is choked out and crickets take up residence. It's time to get to work.

Two sayings prod me along throughout the task. One is the Zen proverb: "Before enlightenment: chop wood, carry water. After enlightenment: chop wood, carry water." And then there's this classic advice to wood stackers everywhere: "Leave space enough for a mouse to get through but not the cat chasing it."

I grouse about the mountain of logs. I bemoan how long it takes to make demonstrable progress. But really, I love the fact that I must stack it well. I cherish the time spent in the flow, finding just the right pieces for the end caps to hold the stacks in place and fitting the hodgepodge of sizes and shapes into a coherent, stable whole. The task at hand forces out other thoughts, and I must dedicate my attention to not dropping logs on my foot, not smashing fingers between logs, and all the while trusting that I am making progress—despite the enormous pile still taunting me.

My daughter has no problem finding her flow space. All I need to do is flip over the logs at the bottom of the pile and she is immediately, totally immersed in exploration and discovery. Crickets, spiders, worms, ants, beetles, centipedes, and unidentifiable bugs and blobs—she adores them all. As I hauled the wood to the pallets the other day, her cries of indignation and disappointment bounce over the swing set. She calls to her brother, "Hey! You didn't even say how beautiful this larva is!"

If only we all could see loveliness in larvae. I would certainly be happier and more contented for it.

Part Two

§

Connection

A Community of Ideas

§

I'VE ALWAYS BEEN OPINIONATED, and I generally savor the opportunity to share my thoughts with others. In 2012, on a lark, I submitted an op-ed to the *Brattleboro Reformer* about a controversial education issue. The piece was well received—a satisfying one-off. Then, unexpectedly, a friend at the *Reformer* mentioned to me that Meg Mott had decided to stop writing her column in order to dedicate herself to finishing a book. This friend asked me to consider filling the spot and encouraged me to call the editor.

I initially balked at the idea of writing every week. I couldn't envision a time when I would fit it in to my schedule; I was concerned that I couldn't think of an interesting topic each week; and, honestly, I felt a little queasy at the thought of sharing so many ideas so publicly. But when the editor offered me the weekly column, the knot in the pit of my stomach— though a sure indication of my nervousness and trepidation— was also a clear sign of excitement and opportunity. It was a defining moment.

Surprisingly, this weekly column has become a vital source of information and communication for me. At first, I mistakenly thought it was all about my thoughts; I've come to realize that, in fact, the column is entirely about this community and the connections we create together.

My readers generally contact me directly, instead of posting to my blog. Every year, hundreds of people reach out to discuss what I've written; they want genuine communication with me about their ideas. Readers e-mail, stop me on the street, send me actual letters, and call me to tell me how something I wrote moved them. They share articles, interviews, links, and YouTube clips—but most importantly, they offer their memories, their confidences, and their principles. This rich exchange of ideas and information has been awe-inspiring. I hold my readers' revelations in profound reverence; they shape who I am and what I yearn for—as a writer, human, and citizen.

It feels entirely fitting that the anniversary of my column frequently coincides with National Library Week. Like my column writ large, our local library is a place where we exchange ideas that are then transformed and transported out into our broader community. And just as my ideas about my writing have shifted as I've crafted my columns all year, how I view our local library has also changed dramatically.

When I was a teenager, our local library was my refuge. Before I had my driver's license, my mom would drop me off, and I'd sit among the stacks for hours, devouring books and periodicals. Likewise, Brooks Memorial Library is a place of solace and shelter for many in our town, as is evident by the patrons who settle in by the windows to read.

A comfortable nostalgia claims me as I watch people reading books and periodicals in the same way I did thirty years ago. But our libraries have become so much more dynamic and powerful than they were when I searched for elements of myself in novels and biographies. They are now pulsating information centers feeding the community's insatiable curiosity.

What hasn't changed is that we unceasingly search for connection and consequence. We seek out information and context to give our lives meaning and direction and to guide us towards our best selves. As was illuminated by a recent study by Pew Research Center for the Pew Internet and American Life Project, libraries have changed because "information is now portable, participatory, and personal." It is the participatory and personal elements that most interest me, as so many people now go to libraries to connect to individuals and organizations through the internet.

More than 99 percent of American libraries provide free internet to their communities. Half of all people who visit American libraries take advantage of that service. Millions of people use it for education and training, as well as for career and employment information. A staggering 84 percent of Americans surveyed said that internet availability at libraries is critically important for their communities. Our libraries facilitate the sharing and consumption of ideas, and anyone can find a point of connection and entry: a recent week's offerings at Brooks Memorial Library included one-on-one computer coaching, a Jane Austen book club discussion, a lecture on American Western art, and an Italian vacation film series. Certainly these offerings encourage edification, but really—at their core—they're about building relationships and bonds in and across our community.

Seth Godin—best-selling author and dynamic entrepreneur—recently posted on his blog about the critical importance of connection: "The next time you feel lonely, disconnected or unappreciated, consider that unlike many other maladies . . . this one is easily overcome by realizing you can cure the problem by connecting, appreciating and leading." When we realize that others need us and "our forward motion, and the value we create," we can assuage our feelings of disconnection. He concludes that when we share the light of new ideas, we all see more clearly.

If you look carefully some afternoon you might see me, like countless others, tapping away on my laptop, crafting my next column in the mezzanine of our local library. That hallowed space evokes and solidifies for me the reason why I write each week; like those others, I too strive to be a point of connection, interaction, and the exchange of ideas and emotions.

A Tale of Four Mowers

❦

I FELT CERTAIN that my neighbors would think I'd replaced my lawn with a wheat crop. This is Vermont, after all, and the idea isn't so very far-fetched. My embarrassingly tall grass had gone to seed, and my earnest people-powered mower was no match for the savannah. April had been so dry and then May suddenly so very wet that I roundly neglected the mowing. With a break in the rain came the resolve that it was time to do battle. But my humble reel mower literally couldn't cut it.

I headed up the hill to visit my neighbors who live by a succulent mulberry tree. They had a mower to lend, but it was notoriously unreliable. My neighbor explained the glitches, crossed her fingers, and bid us good luck. I hauled it home and fired it up as my son watched from his perch in a pine tree. Two rows later, the engine quit. Despite my insistent tugging on its frayed cord, it resisted restarting. And then, when it did finally roar back to life, it wouldn't shut off. The safety bar intended to force an automatic shutdown was on the blink. When we finally got it to stop, we trudged back up the hill to return the dicey device.

Another neighbor was happy to loan us her earnest battery-powered mower. She'd traded in her loud gas-powered one for this sleek, sexy, high-tech green mower. She simply pushed a button and it started! Amazingly quiet and lightweight, it was quite a machine. I was off to tame my wild grasslands—with a mower I could feel sanctimonious about. Two gorgeous sweeps later, it lost all power: dead battery. I considered my lawn. It now looked like a grass maze designed for the neighborhood kids. I needed another mower, another neighbor.

Our new neighbors in the red house were happy to oblige and offered me their reel mower. I shook my head: "Grass is too high." "Scissors?" she joked. I admitted that it just might come to that. She gestured across the street: "Ken's always willing to loan out his mower." But Ken wasn't home, so I trudged home to use own my mower, much like I would a rolling pin. If I couldn't cut the grass, at least I could flatten it and make it less obtrusive.

As I tussled with my mower and felt my biceps twinging from the effort, the new neighbor called from her car: "Ken's home now! You could ask about the mower!" Hallelujah! I ditched the oversized rolling pin and dashed to secure yet another mower. It was a dinosaur of a machine, its grass bag had gone missing years ago, and it weighed about as much as a stegosaurus. But it worked! I grinned as it gobbled. I was so thrilled that I went on to mow my next-door neighbor's expansive lawn. A stay-at-home dad, he very nearly cried when he returned home, his son in his arms, and gazed upon my work. He called out, "I can't thank you enough! You just gave me back my day tomorrow!"

Just recently, I'd frantically e-mailed him and several other neighbors when my family and I headed to New York and had forgotten to turn off our coffee maker. He turned it off for us, but long after the pot was safely disarmed, we continued to receive inquiries from other neighbors about the overheating coffee maker situation.

We have a wonderful neighborhood.

I didn't want to move into this neighborhood—in fact, I swore I *wouldn't* move here. Six years ago the area was decidedly rough around the edges. But there weren't many houses on the market, and at least this house was close to downtown. I was pregnant with our first child and wanted to feel more settled; I didn't want to rent anymore. And—cardinal sin for any homebuyer—we fell in love with the house. Its beautiful, unpainted turn-of-the-century woodwork was stunning, as were its pristine maple floors. We were goners. But I cried a lot that first year. The street noise drove me to distraction, and I feared that our house would never really feel like home.

But as grass clippings spewed all over me from the fourth lawn mower that day, I realized that—to my surprise—I love my neighborhood. Whether we're feeding each other's pets, bringing in mail, looking for missing cats, providing meals when someone dies or is born, gathering a neighbor's maple sap so it doesn't go to waste while she's away, or just leaning over our fence to chat, I feel a kinship with these folks.

Howard Blackson of Placemakers—an influential and successful urban planning firm—articulates what he views as the critical Five C's of what makes a neighborhood great: complete, compact, connected, complex, and convivial. Though I don't doubt the importance of all these components, I think that a neighborhood—regardless of its connection to transit lines or close proximity to good coffee and cozy gathering spots—must first and foremost be caring.

And altruism, it turns out, is contagious. In a first-of-its-kind study completed by researchers at UCLA as well as the University of Cambridge and the University of Plymouth in the UK, researchers found that watching someone help another person triggers that same desire in others. Says lead researcher Simone Schnall of Cambridge, "When you feel this sense of moral 'elevation' not only do you say you want to be a better person and help others, but you actually do when the opportunity presents itself." I've seen this at work in my own neighborhood.

As I headed in to start dinner after my marathon session of searching for mowers, I heard the sound of another mower in our backyard. Our mulberry neighbors, not knowing we'd found a working mower, had jerry-rigged their finicky mower and returned, prepared to mow our lawn themselves.

Exploring the Shortcomings
of Solitude

§

DECEMBER 16, 2014

DURING LAST WEEK'S multi-day sleet, rain, and ice fest, my car slid to a stop at an intersection and I saw a woman walking in the street. This was unsurprising, given the three inches of slush on the sidewalk, but her face was serene—not plastered with the scowl that I'd anticipated. And she was, by my quick, superficial assessment of her clothes and hairstyle, of middle-class means.

As she trod closer, I saw that her pants were rolled above her ankles, and her feet were bare. She confidently strode through freezing rain and ice pellets. I shivered as I watched; her feet were scarlet. I've fabricated a host of scenarios to explain her situation. Did her shoes and socks get so hopelessly soaked that she simply jettisoned them? Was she in the midst of some kind of delusion that allowed her to be so calm? And why didn't I offer her a ride? Her peaceful demeanor was confounding; she did not appear to want help, and I did not wish to intrude on something I did not understand.

We constantly strive to make meaning as we meet people—or simply observe them. We assess, consider, and then, often, categorize. Our evaluations provide a scaffold for understanding someone and incorporating them into our world. But these immediate assessments—devoid of rich and critical context—also limit true connection and understanding. I have an acquaintance who asserts that colleagues often underestimate her worth before they have any real context for understanding her: "I pull up in a mini-van, and I am coded as 'the forty-something mom.'" They construct a story about her life and experiences. She feels misjudged in her intelligence and ability to contribute meaningfully. Eventually, they realize that she listens to every word in every meeting, synthesizes the many details, and makes important observations that few others can.

What if we asked better questions of each other? What if we let our genuine innate curiosity drive real conversations instead of merely a desire to get to the next step in a project? Research shows that conversations aren't just an important tool to build connections; talking with people—even strangers—elevates our own sense of well-being.

Nicholas Epley, a behavioral scientist at the Booth School of Business at the University of Chicago, and a doctoral student, Juliana Shroeder, challenged conventional wisdom about commuters and the unwritten code of bus and train travel: Don't make eye contact and don't talk to one another. They offered $5 gift cards to Chicago commuters. Members of one group had to talk with a stranger during their commute. Another group of straphangers were to follow social norms and not interact with anyone. Those who had conversations with strangers reported having more positive commutes than those who sat in solitude. This contradicted the commuters' own predictions about which situation would be more pleasant.

Elizabeth Dunn of the University of British Columbia and Michael Norton of the Harvard Business School made similar findings in one of their experiments. They asked some Starbucks customers "to have a genuine interaction" with the cashier—to smile and chitchat. Others were instructed to get in and out as efficiently as possible. The talkative dawdlers reported feeling more cheerful than those who kept their interactions brief and businesslike.

As I face the long, dark winter, I plan to employ any means necessary to stave off the doldrums. I plan to linger a bit with cashiers and bank tellers, and I may even stop to chat with strangers on the street. I will cut myself some slack, and I'll do the same for you.

Finding the Overlap

§

JUNE 25, 2013

I KNEW SHE WORKED on the Hill in the House of Representatives, but I didn't know she was a Republican staffer from Kentucky. We'd been accepted to a bipartisan leadership program at Yale University, and we arranged to be roommates. For each of us, the main concern was saving on the cost of a hotel; we hadn't considered our political views. Her train from DC was very late, so there wasn't much time to get to know each other—just enough time to determine that we occupied opposite sides of the political spectrum. We laughed that we'd voluntarily thrown ourselves together: she, twenty years my junior and from a red state that is often the butt of redneck jokes, and I from what many perceive as not just a blue state but a wacky blue state. Before heading to bed, I sent a text message to a friend reporting that my roommate was a southern Republican. Her response: "Ha! Good luck with that!"

I actually loved that we were going to have to make it work.

As we gobbled mini-Danishes and gulped strong coffee at breakfast the next day, we took bolder steps into the topics we'd danced around. She told me that she was a strong fiscal conservative but not a social conservative. "People should marry who they want to," she told me. "It isn't my business to say who you can love."

I smiled and replied, "That's great, because I've got a wife and two kids back home in Vermont."

To her credit, she recovered quickly and said, "Really? Well, that's great."

Once over that hurdle, we got along famously. Because of our ridiculously late nights studying, we had to help each other get out the door prepared and on time. I prompted her to grab her required name tag each day; she reminded me to dab on the deodorant. Deep bonds are necessarily formed when you start talking about armpits.

We certainly had our political disagreements, but this northern Democrat and that southern Republican found enough overlap that we had civil, engaging conversations— and we also laughed uproariously together. Humor unifies. My roomie had me chortling and guffawing late into the night. I cherished the fun she poked at me and my liberal clan. We often lose our sense of humor when discussions devolve into unsavory partisan accusations, but laughter is usually just what we need to bring us back to common ground. And although people often accuse powerful women of lacking a sense of humor, I think talented women leaders tend to see the wisdom and relief found in laughter.

If the GOP is going to have a successful revival, I believe it will be due to its women. In a week in which rising Republican star Marco Rubio threatened to kill an immigration bill if it included Senator Patrick Leahy's amendment to guarantee protections for same-sex partners of immigrants, I met numerous dynamic women Republicans who found his ideological posturing both unhelpful and offensive. They want their party to focus on economics and security.

Lisa Spies, a powerhouse fundraiser for the Republican Party, threw her head back and laughed when she looked at my nametag. "Vermont? I think I know every Republican in Vermont! Last election, my handful of Vermont Republicans kept asking me for Romney signs, but I didn't want to throw money away!" Spies is the go-to gal whenever the Republican Party wants to reach out to Jewish women. She is a charming, funny, and successful anomaly: a Jewish Republican female. I asked her why she raises money for the GOP. Her answer was unequivocal: "I want to do everything I can to defend Israel. Security issues are hugely important to me." For her, the social issues take a backseat. I do not agree with her. I cannot unequivocally support Israel's actions in the West Bank and Gaza, nor can I ignore the ways in which the Republican Party continues to work against my interests as a woman. However, I still think it is important to take the time to listen to others perspectives and opinions.

Similarly, I got to know a Black Republican woman from Alabama. She gets double takes whenever she "comes out" as a Republican. Less polite people smirk and sneer, "How can you possibly be a Republican?" She says her constituents believe the GOP is the party that will address economic worries and she doesn't feel she can overcome this perception. She's committed to trying to change the Republican party from within. She's also pragmatic: She'll never be elected from her district as a Democrat. I met a number of Black women from the Deep South who believed this same thing. Being a woman and being Black was already two strikes against them.

Among my posse for the week there were left- and right-leaning activists from across the nation and the world. A communications director from a GOP caucus in the Midwest became a close friend. Some classmates started referring to us as "Carville and Matalin," after the political odd couple of Democratic strategist James Carville and Republican political consultant Mary Matalin. One day she arrived at our class carrying a complimentary copy of the *Wall Street Journal* from the hotel. "Hey," I complained, "why didn't you grab me one?" She protested that she knew the *New York Times* was my homepage on my computer. I laughed and explained that I read them both: "I have to know what you people are saying about us!" She grinned and nodded.

On my morning run yesterday, I considered the necessity of finding points of agreement. There are always two quite disparate groups out at dawn: smokers and runners. Yet, despite our starkly different motivations for arising at daybreak, we all turn our faces towards the sun, welcoming the promise of a new day.

On Being Neighborly

§

THIS WEEKEND IS MY BIRTHDAY. It is also the anniversary of a more gruesome milestone. May 5, 1945, was the day Mauthausen concentration camp was liberated near Linz, Austria—the birthplace of Adolph Hitler. I know this date—and keep track of it—because my paternal grandfather, Leopold Bálint (Leo to his friends and family), was murdered while on a forced march from Mauthausen to the town of Gunskirchern in the waning days of the Third Reich.

On April 22, only two weeks before the camp's liberation, Leo stopped to assist another ailing prisoner. He knew, as they all did, that stopping along the march meant certain death, but he did what so many others—before and after him—have done. His humanity and empathy overpowered his fear. Leo wrapped this man's arm about his shoulder, put his own arm around the weary man's waist, and dragged him along for a short distance. His already-low reserves were soon spent, and they fell dangerously behind the group. As eyewitnesses informed my grieving grandmother afterwards, both Leo and his comrade were summarily shot and their bodies heaved into the chilly waters of the Danube.

I know Leopold only from the family stories I have heard and from the memoir my father is working valiantly to finish. And yet, this story still gives me an ache in my chest whenever I allow myself the quiet space to think about it. My grandfather's murder impacted so many lives and continues to do so. As Elie Wiesel has written, "Time does not heal all wounds; there are those that remain painfully open."

From my parents I get my sense of humor, my insatiable curiosity, and a deep love of history, but because we have also passed this pain from generation to generation, I am a latecomer to the belief that neighbors can be a force for good in the world. My father was always, and remains, hesitant about connecting with neighbors. I used to chalk it up to European manners, but in my adulthood I have come to realize it is actually a manifestation of the complex trauma of the Holocaust. Of course he doesn't want the neighbors to know too much about him and his family. Neighbors can betray you; indeed they did betray him and his family.

There are stories my dad tells that reveal how his wariness of neighbors took root. There was the time my grandfather had a bathtub installed in their apartment building, and the neighbors all griped that "those dirty, stinking Jews are bathing too much." And the time my dad's postwar neighbors in Germany (who knew that his father had been killed by the Nazis) gave him parts of a Hitler Youth costume to wear for Fasching, a holiday similar to Mardi Gras. Or the worst story of all: the trusted teacher who gathered information from his young students about who had Jewish parents. One ongoing toll of the Holocaust—beyond the destruction of families, the loss of faith, and the enormous grief—is that we start to doubt our neighbors' basic humanity. We come to believe that it is safer to keep them at a distance, because people can be so horribly callous.

How does one recover from the horror and absurdity? I really don't know for certain, but I am trying my best to break this cycle. It helps that Vermont's small-town character makes it a state of neighbors. My dad has come to understand that my family and I love our town and feel safe here, but he still occasionally comments about his personal discomfort with small-town life. He once exclaimed in horror, "Your letter carrier knows where you lived before you moved to this street?" One of the first things he asked when we bought our house in town was: How are the neighbors? Will they be kind to you? Will they accept your family?

Daniel Goldhagen argued in his controversial book *Hitler's Willing Executioners: Ordinary Germans and the Holocaust* (1996) that ordinary Germans were willing and eager to participate in the so-called Final Solution because German culture and society had indoctrinated them in "eliminationist anti-Semitism." Although many historians (Americans, Germans, and Israelis among them) excoriated the book, maintaining that Goldhagen's research was shoddy and that he ignored any material that did not prove his thesis, he still became something of a celebrity on his German book tour. Despite its academic shortcomings, his book resonated with many Germans who understood that Hitler's ghastly plans were only set in motion because average people chose to look the other way.

When faced with stories of atrocity and bravery, we often ask ourselves: Would I have had the courage to stand up and do the right thing? But I think that this is perhaps the wrong question because most of us will never be faced with such a situation. Instead, the real question is: Do I have the courage, day in and day out, to show kindness to and concern for my neighbors? The small gestures do really matter. When I bake bread for a neighbor (even if our politics don't match) or check on another when she's sick (although she sometimes talks my ear off), I am asserting that there is still basic humanity in the world. I do it for me, for my parents, for my children, and for their great-grandfather, Leopold Bálint, who retained his humanity in the midst of the Holocaust.

Point of Impact

§

JULY 23, 2013

W̲E̲'̲D̲ ̲H̲E̲A̲R̲ ̲T̲H̲E̲ ̲J̲A̲R̲R̲I̲N̲G̲ ̲R̲O̲A̲R̲ and screech of the garbage truck mid-breakfast. My son's eyes would grow as large as cereal bowls and he'd yelp: "Trash truck!" (For the longest time he could not articulate the "tr" consonant combination, so he developed a clicking sound similar to the language of the Dobe !Kung people of the Kalahari Desert.) He'd click and we'd dash out the door—I in my untied shoes; he bobbing up and down in his backpack and pajamas and unkempt hair. We'd follow that truck (and the accompanying stench) on its appointed rounds each Monday more faithfully than a Saint Bernard on the trail of a mountain rescue. My son loved everything about it: the noise, the lights, the hydraulic rams that crushed the oozing mess, and all the "treasures" we'd find along the curbs. It was how we started each week for a good year.

Then Waste Management out of Keene, New Hampshire, lost the bid for the contract to handle Brattleboro's trash, and

I knew that a new crew would soon be doing the runs. On what I thought might be their last day, my son and I were late getting out the door. We chased that truck from South Main to Canal to Fuller Street, where we finally—and triumphantly—caught up with it and waved a cheery greeting to the crew. Unexpectedly, the driver and his helper stopped their work, and the driver called out: "We were afraid we wouldn't see you today. It's our last day, you know." His helper reached into the truck's cab, pulled out a bright green plush toy, and handed it to my son. It was a garbage truck that made crushing and beeping noises when you grabbed its middle. "We were sad to lose the bid," he said. "We're going to miss that little guy."

WE GO THROUGH OUR DAYS, the days stretch to years, and we are often dismayed that we're not having an impact at all in this world. When that worker handed that toy to my son, I understood humanity and connection in a new and entirely palpable way. We'd never spoken to that crew except to wave and smile as we watched them work each Monday, but our presence alone, and the implied appreciation for their work, made a difference. Certainly, it also changed us. Hell, I set my watch by their schedule—it was that important to my son.

Of course, our unintended impact is not always a positive one. I have a friend who still remembers when a teacher at a competitive dance camp dashed her hopes of strutting in the footlights when she bellowed, "I don't know what you're trying to do, but you look like a wilted palm tree!" Perhaps meant to inspire, it instead caused my friend to abandon her dreams.

She laughs about the comment now, but she also acknowledges that that was the moment when she gave up on a dance career.

Part of the impact others have on us is simply a cellular-level reaction. V. S. Ramachandran—distinguished professor of neuroscience at the University of California, San Diego—asserts that mirror neurons enable us to feel what others feel and are the basis of human empathy. Have you ever felt yourself break into a smile simply by watching someone else smile? Or have you ever watched someone get hurt and then you recoiled automatically in sympathy? Scientists believe that mirror neurons are why we react immediately, instinctively, and involuntarily to others' actions.

Neuroscientists Giacomo Rizzolatti and Vittorio Gallese and their colleagues at the University of Parma in Italy first identified the presence of mirror neurons by studying the premotor cortex of macaque monkeys. They noticed that the same neurons fired when the monkeys grabbed a peanut and also when they simply watched another monkey grab a peanut. To confirm the presence of mirror neuron systems in humans, multiple studies have used functional magnetic resonance imaging (fMRI) to image brain activity. One study examined the brain activity of participants while they observed experimenters make finger motions and as they made those same movements themselves; the same areas of the frontal cortex and the parietal lobule were active in both situations.

There is much debate about the real significance of the discovery of mirror neurons. In an article for the University of California, Berkeley, magazine *Greater Good: The Science of a Meaningful Life*, author Jason Marsh calls Ramachandran one of mirror neurons' "most ardent champions." He quotes Ramachandran from the Being Human Conference in San Francisco in 2012 dismissing the notion that mirror neurons have gotten too much publicity: "I don't think they're being exaggerated, I think they're being played down, actually." Ramachandran believes they are nothing less than the basis of human empathy—and by extension, human civilization.

Whether mirror neurons are, in fact, "the single most important unpublicized story of the decade," as Ramachandran asserts, or if their discovery is simply one important piece of an exceedingly complex understanding of human empathy, there's no doubt that our gestures, our words, and our actions and reactions have an impact on those around us. When we own the fact that we have an impact on others—whether we intend to or not—we are one step closer to purposefully crafting our effect on others.

As I wearily jogged up South Main the other day, past grimy clusters of garbage cans and recycling bins, an elderly man stopped, grinned, and tipped his hat to me. Despite my fatigue, I immediately smiled back and suddenly found that energy I needed for that last burst up the hill.

At the Finish Line

§

WE FIRST HEARD the devastating news about the Boston Marathon bombing through the anxious messages my father-in-law left on our answering machine.[2*] Knowing that we're runners, he thought we might have been at the Marathon—either running or cheering on friends. As he is not a runner himself, he can be forgiven for not knowing that we'd never achieve the qualifying times required to toe the starting line of running's most hallowed race. And as a non-runner friend recently confided to my spouse about having to watch her husband's races, "Running is not a terribly exciting event to watch." It's a lot of standing around waiting for your loved one to dash (or lope) past.

That is what I've been thinking about this week: cheering on runners—especially those you don't know personally—is a selfless public show of love and support for other people. It is an act that demonstrates admiration for those who push

---

[2*] The Boston Marathon bombing occurred on April 15, 2013. Terrorists planted two pressure-cooker bombs near the finish line, killing three and injuring hundreds.

beyond their self-conceived limits; it confirms the resilience and aspirations of humankind. Those spectators in Boston who found themselves dreadfully close to ground zero represent the best parts of all of us. They stood in solidarity with strength and hope, and as a result, their pain and horrific loss is not theirs alone.

I ran my first distance race—the Leaf Peepers Half Marathon in Waterbury, Vermont—almost a decade ago. As a lifelong asthmatic, I never thought I could run that far. But I picked up a dog-eared training guide at a used bookshop and decided I could do it if I simply followed the advice of the author, Olympic marathon runner Jeff Galloway: Adhere to the "one more mile" philosophy. Each week, you add just one more mile to your longest run, and eventually—miraculously—you work your way up to the desired total. I was simultaneously skeptical and hopeful.

That summer, I logged a lot of miles along Putney's back roads and was astounded when I soon routinely ran for over an hour without collapsing in a foul, sweaty heap. Galloway later developed a more specific training program for novice distance runners like me, but the advice I followed that summer was bare-boned. Bottom line: I really didn't know what the hell I was doing. This meant that I didn't drink enough water; I didn't consume enough calories; I ran too many hills and injured both of my Achilles tendons. I confided to one of my friends that I often felt queasy at the end of my long runs. She declared that I certainly needed more food and water. I insisted that it had more to do with the heat, or my asthma medicine, or my speed—pretty much anything other than the obvious factors.

And yet I kept at it. It was so satisfying to push my body far beyond what I had believed possible. In my mind, I was still that chubby, ten-year-old asthmatic, wheezing and crying on my family's back stoop because I couldn't catch my breath after a rowdy game of touch football with the neighborhood kids. My body's transformation happened a lot more quickly than my spirit's. It was only when I stood at the starting line that following autumn that I finally began to see myself in a different light. I allowed myself to believe: *I am a runner.*

I wish I could report that my first race was triumphant. I wish I could recount my perfectly executed race plan and my soaring feelings of invincibility. In fact, though, it was pretty ugly. As many inexperienced runners do, I went out too fast. An awful stomach cramp gripped me mid-race, and by mile 10 I was undeniably starving. Other runners had wisely packed sports gels and hip flasks of Gatorade. I could only gulp entirely unsatisfying water from minuscule cups at each hydration station and search my psyche for the will to keep hobbling along.

I had a lot of help along the way, however. Other runners offered encouragement and advice as they shuffled by, their comments devoid of judgment or disparagement. Everyone who passed me seemed entirely invested in my completion of this small, inconsequential race. So I had to finish; I couldn't let them down.

The last quarter mile passed through the aging stubble of a cornfield whose edge was framed by a tiny ditch—the very one I had to ford in order to reach the finish line's chute. But this modest drainage trench took on mammoth proportions in my mind. My legs were useless—rubbery like the appendages of an octopus—entirely unsuited for running a half marathon. I feared the trough would be my undoing. But as I willed my jelly legs to buck up, I heard the spectators cheering on the runners ahead of me.

They were not hailing the winners. No, the fleet of foot had finished a full hour earlier. Now they were applauding the poor, gutsy slobs like me who had once thought that a half marathon sounded like a good idea. Their boisterous cheers and clanging cowbells nearly brought me to tears. I knew I would finish. There is, of course, high drama that plays out on any racecourse. There are photo finishes and come-from-behind victories. There are first-time finishers who revel in their achievements, and extraordinarily devoted parents who push wheelchair-bound children along for 26.2 backbreaking miles. But there is nothing so dramatic, or so noble, as the throngs of supporters who welcome us all home for no reason but love.

Rendering Assistance
to Someone in Need

§

MAY 31, 2018

HAVE YOU SEEN the absolutely riveting video of Mamoudou Gassama—a Malian man living in France—who scaled four stories on the outside of an apartment building to rescue a young boy dangling from a balcony? Gassama said he saw the child in peril and knew exactly what he had to do. "I wasn't thinking about being brave," Gassama said afterwards. "I had to save him."

I've often thought about these dramatic, harrowing moments and what compels a person to act. But I've come to realize that all of us are constantly being tested in thousands of less spectacular interactions.

Early one weekend morning last month, I headed out for a hike. My dog bounded ahead, and moments later, I could hear him barking furiously. I assumed it was a porcupine lumbering through a hemlock grove. But when I careened around the curve, I thought I spied a pile of old clothes in the trail.

But then I noticed legs. And arms. It was a man, lying face down in the trail. The night had been below freezing, and my first thought was that he'd died of exposure. My heart was pounding as I observed him, and I was extremely relieved when he began to move. He'd burrowed into his T-shirt and hoodie in an attempt to keep warm, and now he was all tangled up in them and couldn't find his sleeves. My dog's barking scared him, and he began to cry.

As I tried to calm the dog and the man, I became aware of my own position of vulnerability. I'm slight—just five feet tall and ninety-eight pounds. And I was out in the woods, early in the morning, with a complete stranger. He seemed emotionally fragile, and I had a dog with me for protection. Yet I still felt small and scared. He was an entirely unknown quantity.

He told me that he'd lost his way back to his makeshift campsite in the woods the night before, and through tears he asked if I would help him find his stuff. The next hour was full of constant calculation: How exactly could I help? What were the maximum and minimum levels of engagement that I felt comfortable offering? I wanted to give both compassion and real assistance. And I didn't want to be cavalier about my own safety. I felt the same kind of hyper-vigilance and adrenaline that I had experienced when I was a Wilderness First Responder.

I jogged back to my car to get a spare coat and hat for him, and when I returned, I gathered information about his life, his situation, and what had led up to him being alone in the woods. Together, we made a plan to get him into Brattleboro for some food and to find him more secure shelter. With assistance from friends and professionals in town, we made sure he had a safe place, at least in the short term. As we carried out the plan, he kept asking me, "Why are you helping me?" I'd reply, "You're a human being and you need help." He'd say, "But you don't know me." At one point I got teary and said, "You could be my own brother. I'd want someone to be there for him."

The moments that test us and our compassion are almost certainly a mix of doubt, concern, dread, sadness, fear, love—a confusion of emotions. And the assistance in the moment, although crucial, does not alter the massive structural deficits that contribute to any individual experiencing a crisis. Helping this person find a safe place in the short term will not alleviate the shortage of affordable housing needed for more long-term support. But my work in this world is both things: legislative work to change the structures and personal work to help alleviate immediate suffering.

Addressing Bias Starts Within

§

MY PREVIOUS COLUMN, "Rendering Assistance to Someone in Need," resonated deeply with so many readers. Due to a looming deadline and space constraints, I streamlined the story and left out details. I knew that I couldn't adequately explore them in one column. But nuance is always important.

I had come upon a man in the woods who desperately needed help. I excluded from the first column that he was a Black man. I mention it now because the man's skin color and my own—and our different personal experiences in the world—clearly affected our interactions.

When my dog first came upon him, I feared that the man might have died of exposure. But the dog's frantic barking roused him. As I pulled the dog away, he called after me, "I know you're scared of me. I know I'm scary." He said this even though *we* had clearly frightened *him;* the dog was threatening, and perhaps he thought it would bite.

I tried to reassure him that we—my dog and I—were just startled. But, honestly, I was scared. And I know enough about implicit bias to understand that this was at least part of the unease I felt.

This past biennium, Representative Diana Gonzalez and I organized a workshop for legislators and statehouse staff to explore the issue of implicit bias—the attitudes or stereotypes that affect our understanding, actions, and decisions in an unconscious manner. The associations we hold in our subconscious develop over the course of a lifetime through our direct life experiences as well as messages imbedded in millions of bits of information from news clips, books, movies, television, and social media. This onslaught of information creates unconscious feelings about other people based on characteristics such as race, ethnicity, age, and appearance.

In that moment, I reminded myself of my own implicit bias, and this awareness helped me to navigate my intense emotions as I tried to help him.

We decided to get him into town for a hot beverage and some food. While we drove, we chatted, and I made a plan. This happened right around the time that two Black men were arrested for merely sitting in a Starbucks. I didn't want him to have a similarly awful experience, but I knew I needed to leave his side while I sought additional help from professionals in our community.

After bringing him to a café and giving him some money, I told the workers at the counter that he was with me. I also explained that he was a bit agitated and disoriented and that he might be there awhile as I called the folks at Groundworks, the local resource center for people facing housing and food insecurity. I was conscious of the fact that I was worried about how he'd be treated because of his skin color. It's critical that we acknowledge bias—both explicit and implicit—and work hard to combat it, both societally and within ourselves.

As I write this, President Trump has spoken about immigrants from Central America as vermin that "infest" our county. *The Washington Post*'s editorial board's response, a piece entitled "Repugnant," pulled no punches: "Mr. Trump's policy for the past weeks has been repugnant, reprehensible, and repulsive. It could be justified only by those who view Salvadorans and Hondurans not as humans who deserve to live but as animals—as pests—who 'infest.'"

The editorial is spot on. But I want us all—even as we fight President Trump and his administration's lies about immigration that dehumanize and spread fear—to acknowledge that we must each do the day-to-day work required to change the culture in which such abhorrent ideas take root. Sometimes the work required of us presents itself in a chance meeting in the woods.

Stories as Scaffolding

§

JUNE 24, 2014

WE TELL A STORY in my family about when my siblings and I started to finish the sentences of docents at historic sites throughout the Northeast. By the time we were all in elementary school, we could recite many a spiel given by eager interpreters of colonial objects and lifestyles of early America's rich and famous. At one site—perhaps famed Revolutionary War general Philip J. Schuyler's home in Albany, New York—our chipper guide made the stale joke about the metal bed warmer being a colonial popcorn maker. My sister first displayed her jaundiced eye and then launched her deadpan unequivocal response: "Nope. It's a bed warmer." Looking back, I imagine that poor museum worker—dressed in period costume, no doubt, and probably feeling decidedly vulnerable in her silly dust cap—sizing up my family and thinking, *Who are these people?*

While other families took vacations to the beach or Disneyland, my family only ventured to holiday "destinations" at which we could "learn something." After visiting the colonial-era homes of prominent English and Dutch individuals all along the Eastern Seaboard, we branched out to Revolutionary and Civil War battlefields and monuments, then important whaling and fishing communities, all the while stopping at each and every historic marker and statue along the way. Although my parents claim I suffered from terrible motion sickness in the car, I think that most of the problem was the constant stopping and starting as we sought to edify ourselves at each roadside placard commemorating important local events: "James Fenimore Cooper may have stayed at an inn that possibly once stood on this spot. It is believed that he might have penned a few pages of his *Leatherstocking Tales* here."

Although we vigorously advocated for more "normal" getaways involving sand, sun, and amusement parks, there's no denying that these educational jaunts provided us with a lot of great comic material and undoubtedly shaped our interests as well as our aesthetic sense.

Best-selling author and *New York Times* columnist Bruce Feiler asserts that these experiences and family stories also provide children, including me and my siblings, with tools that makes us more resilient. Feiler's curiosity about what makes some children more equipped to overcome adversity than others led him to research conducted by psychologist Marshall Duke at Emory University. Duke's work indicates that one key to strengthening families is to help your children develop a strong family narrative.

Duke's wife, Sara—a psychologist who works with children with learning disabilities—noticed an interesting phenomenon in her practice. "The ones who know a lot about their families," she observed, "tend to do better when they face challenges." Intrigued by Sara's hypothesis, Duke teamed up with fellow Emory psychology professor Robyn Fivush to test it out. Eventually, Fivush and Duke developed a simple measure, the "Do You Know?" scale, which has twenty questions to determine a child's sense of family. Children were asked an assortment of questions about their families and their own personal histories: Do you know your birth story? Do you know where your parents met? Do you know of an illness or something really bad that happened to your family?

In the summer of 2001, when they interviewed families about these questions and then compared the children's answers to their results from a battery of psychological tests, the correlation was astonishing: children who knew more about their own personal history and their family's narrative had a much stronger sense of control over their lives and had higher self-esteem.

Fivush and Duke's theory was unexpectedly tested further following the terrorist attacks of September 11, 2001. The researchers went back to the same families and re-interviewed the children in the midst of this national trauma. "Once again," Duke explains, "the ones who knew more about their families proved to be more resilient, meaning they could moderate the effects of stress." These children have an understanding of their family's "unifying narrative," and this provides them with what Duke and Fivush refer to as "an intergenerational self"—a strong sense that they are part of something larger than themselves.

Although constructing a strong family narrative with your children is crucial, the type of story line you create is also important. Some families have an ascending family story: "We used to be so poor but now we have made it." Other families have a descending one: "Your great grandfather made a lot of money selling real estate. But then he lost it all, and we've struggled ever since." But the narrative that best creates a sense of family resilience and spirit is one that fluidly fluctuates between the two: "We've had our ups and downs, good times and bad times, but through it all we support each other."

Like my own family's outings to view an endless string of early American bed warmers, hokey family trips and traditions seem to be some of the inexplicable glue that binds kin together. The amusing anecdotes about my siblings correcting the museum guides become much more than droll recollections: they themselves became part of our family narrative and further enhanced our family's identity as a unit that is able to overcome adversity.

I'm still unpacking from last week's trip to Mystic Seaport, where we dragged the kids to see interpreters hauling up the yard on an 1880s three-masted square-rigged ship as salty sea chanteys rang out across the water. No doubt my own kids will soon develop practiced eye-rolling as eager docents interrogate them about rigging, bowsprits, and capstans. I imagine I will smile when that happens, knowing that we've created memories that fastened us tightly together like the hundreds of strands that make up the sturdy mainstay.

The Dance of the Excavators

§

JUNE 18, 2013

THE PHALANX of formidable earthmovers parked in front of the old Kipling cinema days before any demolition began. Whenever we passed the captivating sight my children reminded me that they wanted to watch the deconstruction. So, each day, on the way—well, out of the way—to my kids' preschool, we'd check to see if the annihilation had begun. One much-anticipated day, we were treated to the start of the delightful dance of the excavators. We returned each weekday morning until the utterly charmless building became a Brattleboro memory.

Tyler Excavation's exceedingly tidy, efficient work enthralled me. My own day job—parenting—is never tidy, nor is it efficient. And unlike the drivers of these colossal machines, my talents are not nearly so readily apparent—at least to me. It's tough being a parent when you tend towards perfectionism. You focus on daily defeats: my kids enjoy teasing each other so much that I feel like I'm watching Elizabethan bear baiting. You forget to celebrate victories: both my children know the basics of making bread and cleaning a toilet—not simultaneously, of course. And although at times I feel like I live with miniature tyrants, they both can tell a joke and demonstrate love and empathy towards one another. Really, what more could I want? Turns out, a lot.

I want my daily parenting choreography to look more like the Russian Bolshoi Ballet—full of grace and inspiration—and less like Australia's contemporary dance troupe called Chunky Move. In a Chunky Move piece, you are likely to see lights flashing incongruently while someone writhes on the floor—not unlike bedtime at our house. It is the surreal aspect of parenting that I did not anticipate. Exactly how does one maintain lucidity when your two-year-old shrieks for no apparent reason while your five-year-old flips out because you bought the wrong kind of oat cereal? (Never mind that this was the only brand he would eat for the last five months; now it is cereal non grata in the house.)

I'm not alone in feeling like the sanity train left the station a long time ago.

A new Gallup poll in which 60,000 US women were interviewed indicates that stay-at-home moms report more depression, anger, and sadness than moms employed outside the home. They are also more likely to describe themselves as "struggling" and less likely to say they are "thriving." Stay-at-home moms are also less likely to report that they "learned something new today." As a friend of mine who holds a doctorate in psychology says: "When I was at home with the kids, I felt like I was earning a PhD in poop. It was brutal."

The poll only surveyed stay-at-home moms, but several candid conversations I've had with two stay-at-home dads suggest that they experience the same emotional struggles. Parenting is arduous and often lonely. Despite our best efforts, many of us still feel like we're not doing a very good job. When we're not feeling guilty about that or wishing we had superhuman powers, we often feel like we're trapped in an Edvard Munch tableau.

We admonish ourselves for feeling what we feel, though of course we ought to be ever grateful for the opportunity to be home with our children. And I am grateful; I recognize that, in many families, neither parent has the luxury of staying home. But there's a certain weird quality to stay-at-home parenting that challenges rationality.

I once attended a friend's modern dance performance in which the troupe engaged in a type of dance move that she called "sloughing." Like a flake of dead skin peeling from a body, one dancer comes into contact with another one and then "sloughs" off onto the floor. The dance piece was, frankly, kind of weird. Although it made a big impression at the time—not entirely positive, mind you—I secreted it away in some nether region of the brain. There it stayed for seventeen years. But recently I found myself mining this dormant memory when my incensed daughter adhered herself to my leg so that I couldn't walk and then slid down my appendage as if it were a firefighter's pole. I imagined us as participants in a modern dance performance—and not actually part of a frustrating and odd parenting moment. Somehow this made the whole incident more bearable.

WE CONTINUE TO WATCH the site preparation for the new Aldi supermarket. As we enjoy the dance of the excavators each day, I think of our own building project. Together, my kids and I are constructing a home in which my love for them and their interests must blend with my desperate need to learn something new. This is why I sit at the construction site for a few minutes each morning and ponder how the whole marvelous, orderly project fits together.

Our own choreography is often awkward and anything but straightforward. It careens towards bizarre in its banal repetition and is often coupled with my kids' unpredictable, frenzied outbursts of indignation. But this dance we do, full of chunky and clunky movements, has its own grace: an inimitable beauty found in the wonder of the ordinary.

The Grizzled Guys

§

I AM ASHAMED TO ADMIT IT, but I have not always been entirely egalitarian when doling out a "Hi" or "Hello" to a stranger on the street. I tend to smile and engage with folks I deem to be somewhat like myself or those I think have an "open" face. I'm inclined to get that detached, instantaneous "faraway look" when I approach someone I find intimidating. I may be put off by a stranger's dirty clothes, unkempt hair, or pronounced scowl. I sometimes make a quick judgment about income or mental health. Whatever the tiny red flag, I immediately put distance between myself and the stranger. I noticed this pattern on my early morning runs this spring. And it bothered me.

When you run at dawn, there are not many legitimate reasons for not smiling at someone you pass. There are no throngs on the street to wade through; no traffic to demand your attention. Your approach is announced by your rhythmic footfalls and robust intakes of breath. The stranger glances up to satisfy curiosity and to potentially engage; you instantly make your choice. Is this person in need of (or—alternatively—worthy of) a kind greeting? I used to make this calculation all the time, and then I loathed my arbitrary and cruel reckoning. I changed my strategy this April as buds emerged on tender shoots. Like the tiny acts of renewal all around me, I sought a new spring within myself. I now greet everyone in much the same way I welcome the day—with an underlying trust in the goodness that lies at the heart of civility.

The dawn beckons dog walkers, runners, bikers, and elderly folks out for a morning constitutional. It also calls forth those for whom the night is one more trial to be endured. The supple, tender light at the horizon's rim signals a respite from the murky chill; it invites us into optimism and anticipation. One foggy morning, I noticed weary men emerge from alleyways and alcoves in town. Some clutched plastic bags stuffed with necessities, other shuffled along with walking sticks. They nodded greetings and called to each other across Main Street—this clan of grizzled, street-smart men.

I initially felt fear. Having been mugged before, I am not so naïve to believe in my invincibility. And although I was referred to as "Mighty Mite" by college friends, I am still only ninety-eight pounds soaking wet; I know my physical limitations. Next I felt concern: Who are these unfortunate souls who hunker down in Brattleboro's recesses each night? But tucked into my empathy and worry was something I was not eager to admit: I placed these men in a separate category in my mind. They were people to be pitied, not connected to.

Day after day I passed these men. The more I looked into their faces and smiled, the more human they became to me.

My smiles turned into "Hellos," and my hellos evolved into more effusive salutations. Eventually I stopped to exchange names with one man who always greeted me at the corner of High and Main. I wish I could claim that my own progressive, evolved values were responsible for my change. But really, it was memory.

As the sun sidled over the crown of Wantastiquet Mountain one morning, I recalled the story of Philadelphian Anne Mahlum's daybreak runs in 2007. She'd jog past the same group of homeless men in front of the Sunday Breakfast Rescue Mission and wave hello. After weeks of this, she decided to invite these strangers to run with her. That first run included nine homeless men, ages twenty-eight to fifty-seven. Now her nonprofit, Back on My Feet, has chapters in ten American cities.

Through group running, program support, and personal goal setting, her organization helps homeless men and women get their lives back on track. After thirty days of sobriety and another thirty days of running with a team, each member gains access to financial and housing assistance, employment guidance, and training. As fitness and health improve, so does a member's self-perception. Almost 80 percent of program members report that they are certain they will get a job they like, and 94 percent are now hopeful about their future. Almost a thousand members now have gainful employment, and hundreds are in their own apartments.

When Mahlum first pitched her idea, people told her: "These guys aren't going to want to run. They have other things to worry about." Mahlum recalls that "they weren't thought to be deserving of the luxury when they have so much else going on." But Mahlum, an admitted addictive personality herself, knew that her unlikely running mates should not be judged only by appearance, hardships, and addictions, but by their full human measure.

Anne Mahlum never intended to start a nonprofit. You could say that her great idea started with a simple "Hello." But, truly, it began with her critical decision to see people beyond their trappings and cherish not just their basic humanity but their immense potential.

How many such opportunities do we miss? How many grand ideas never come to fruition because we simply look past the grizzled men as they shuffle by?

The Ultimate Improv

§

A FRIEND IS DYING. I had been so certain that she'd managed to whip her cancer that I felt utterly ambushed by the news that it had returned for another grueling contest. And I was wholly unprepared for her decision not to fight this round. So this is where we are: a friend is dying. I have held her spirit close these past few days, and a precious cache of images has opened up to me.

Each fall, we plant a riot of tulips in our front bed. We made a decision years ago that this rather expensive gesture gave so much back to us, to our neighbors, and to passersby, that the investment is absolutely worth it. As I anticipate the sturdy and insistent flowers bursting through the soil and declaring, "Ha! We're here!," I think of my friend skidding to a halt in front of our house, leaning out the window of her car, and yelling, "Love those tulips!" She more than appreciates our tulips—she relishes them. I will savor their lush splendor in a new way this season because, through her simple unabashed pleasure, she has invited me to do so.

My kids have spent hundreds (perhaps thousands?) of hours becoming one with their sandbox. Spring, summer, and fall have meant one thing for years: the sand will inexorably find its way into every nether nook and distant cranny of our home. One of the first phrases my son learned and robustly repeated was one he heard so often from us: "Oh, man! Sand!" Whenever I've doubted the wisdom of inviting the unrelenting Sahara into our home ad infinitum, my friend has been there to insist that kids must be outside. Period. Her no-nonsense attitude leaves little room for argument. I find this such a comfort; we all want to feel that we've made sound parenting decisions.

In hundreds of bits of conversation over the years, she has simply and exquisitely appreciated my parenting. She notices when I strap my kids into backpacks or strollers, unfailingly valuing the beauty in the humble act of getting my children out in the open air. So often my mornings have been filled with her indisputable and fervent words: "It's going to be a beautiful day! You've got to get those kids out!" I hold her broad and adamant smile in my mind's eye as I embark on the daunting struggle with toddlers and their shoes, coats, hats, and mittens. Got to get those kids out. I am profoundly grateful for her resolute articulation of this imperative.

We have spent snatches of many early mornings talking local politics, discussing lines from my column, and swapping parenting stories. Several weeks ago, she shared this chestnut with me. When her daughter was very young, they were out shopping together, and her daughter noticed a haggard mom pushing a shopping cart brimming with children of all ages and sizes. Her daughter turned to her and said, "Mom, these Vermonters just keep having babies until they get a good one, huh?" This story, which made me howl with laughter, now holds special meaning to me; that little girl is now a grown woman who will soon watch her mother let go and fall into the waiting arms of a loving universe.

As I swim in the shock and sorrow of losing my friend, what I've been considering is how love is the ultimate improvisation. Like a jazz pianist who tickles out a melody and waits for the response from the rest of the trio, we throw out riffs and phrases to seek connection with others. We noodle and jam throughout our days and hope to find a groove that sticks. Whether it's screaming, soul-aching love; unfathomable and fierce love for a child; or tender friendships that build slowly over time, we all make it up as we go along. The improvisation is sometimes buoyant and brilliant but just as likely to be clunky and challenging. But we play it, nonetheless, endlessly seeking connection and meaning—fervently wishing to be seen, heard, and, ultimately, remembered.

The devastating news about my friend's cancer coincided with my rediscovery of legendary jazz pianist Bill Evans. The dazzling recordings he made at the Village Vanguard have played nonstop in my kitchen for weeks while I furtively grab snatches of culture between distinctly underwhelming chores. Evans once said, "Each day becomes all of life in microcosm." Although he was referring to the cycle of death and transfiguration that he experienced through his drug addiction, he was onto something much deeper. Whether it is creating unforgettable music or building love one conversation at a time, today is all of life. Our daily experiences create our memory, and our memory, in turn, forges our identity.

In their 2001 book *A General Theory of Love,* Thomas Lewis, Fari Amini, and Richard Lannon, professors of psychiatry at University of California San Francisco, proclaim: "*Memory* is a small word that contains whole worlds." With little effort, we recall places and people long since gone because their impressions remain embedded along our synaptic paths. They explain, "Memory lies at the heart of who we are and who we become. A scientific theory of memory is therefore a map of the soul."

Our memories, then, give us inexhaustible access to all the past improvisation we've created with dear ones—when we composed our love one brave note at a time. And they affirm that our lives are unquestionably richer for all the phrases and refrains we've played together.

Try Gratitude

ॐ

MAKING MY ROUNDS to drop the kids at school each morning, I pause to wave at each volunteer crossing guard. On especially frigid mornings, I fling a vigorous wave, and not just an anemic royal one, towards these altruistic souls. Recently my six-year-old son asked, "Mom, why do you always do that?" I told him that it's simply my way of saying "Good morning!" In a deeper sense, I explained, it is how I express to them my heartfelt appreciation: "I see you there, doing what you're doing, and I am grateful." Without fail, the older gentleman stationed at Elliot and Union and the other posted at Union and Western wave back and flash a cheery grin. I imagine each is thinking, "Thank you for seeing me here." I love the ritual of it: making genuine eye contact with another human being first thing in the morning. Through such effortless gestures, I strengthen the tenuous connections that exist between nameless strangers and me as we face the day's certain labor and its possible delights. We are here. Together.

No matter how irritated I feel in the moments before my wave, I invariably feel better afterwards. The argument with my three-year-old daughter over why she can't be Lady Godiva and go to preschool naked, and the agonizing cajoling with my six-year-old to please, *please*, PLEASE back away from his perfectly arranged Playmobil woolly mammoth setup (complete with Lascaux-esque cave drawings) all fade away. I am still, at heart, an impatient former New Yorker who struggles to keep my lurking aggravation in check, but that daily moment of frank human connection forces me to acknowledge that, no matter how harried I feel, there is always time for respect and kindness.

In that initial hour after "thanking" the crossing guards for their service, I am a happier, more contented driver. I am apt to pause and let drivers stuck at Citizens Bridge pull out onto Western Avenue, or I might slow down to signal to a driver on Putney Road that she can pull out from the Marina entrance. I assure you, this is not my usual driving mode; I am often the one scolding hesitant drivers: "Commit, would you?!" Research on gratitude supports my hunch that expressing thanks helps me feel more positive and relaxed.

Dr. Robert E. Emmons of the University of California, Davis, and Dr. Michael E. McCullough of the University of Miami, who have done the bulk of the current research on gratitude, asked participants in a study to jot down a few reflections each week in a journal. One group was specifically asked to write about what they were grateful for; another recorded what irritated them; the third could write about any events of the previous week that affected them, either positively or negatively. Ten weeks later, the ones who wrote about gratitude were more optimistic, reported feeling happier about their lives, and were healthier; they also exercised more and had fewer doctor's visits than those who'd exclusively written about their aggravations.

Dr. Martin Seligman at the University of Pennsylvania—whom I've referenced before in this column—researched the impact of several different positive psychology interventions on more than 400 participants. Each intervention was compared to a control assignment of simply writing about early memories. When participants were asked to personally deliver a note expressing their gratitude to someone who'd never been adequately thanked for their thoughtfulness, participants' happiness scores shot up. The influence lasted for over a month; it was the most effective positive psychology intervention of any of those tested.

I have experienced the deepest gratitude when I have felt the most vulnerable. Once, when my whole family was sick, I had to schlep the kids to the store to buy a few staples. The checkout clerk—sensing both my misery and exhaustion—was so kind that I nearly cried. Another time I felt sheer panic in the pediatrician's office as I tried to comfort my alarmingly feverish son while keeping my fidgety daughter occupied. The doctor and nurses were entirely professional, yes. But it was the tenderness with which they cared for all of us that touched me. In both of these instances, the act of writing a thank-you card declared my acknowledgment that I am grateful they are in the world. I have never once regretted sending a thank-you note.

Although it is satisfying and rewarding to express thanks to a stranger, a friend, or an acquaintance, it is just as important to adequately thank those who work for you. Not surprisingly, employees work harder for those who show gratitude. A study at the Wharton School at the University of Pennsylvania found that university fundraisers who were told by their boss that she was personally grateful for their hard work made 50 percent more fundraising calls than those who did not receive a message of gratitude. This is not shocking: it feels good to be thanked for our efforts.

I am imperfect, despite my regimen of "thank yous." I can still be impatient and judgmental, moody and intense. I make mistakes and say things I shouldn't. At times I expect too much of my kids and myself. But despite my shortcomings— or perhaps because of them—I am dogged in my commitment to gratitude. Tomorrow morning, as I once again scramble to get my boisterous rapscallions into the car, I know that at the corner of Elliot and Union I will gladly take a brief respite and enjoy the opportunity to wave "Thank you!"

Part Three

&

Vulnerability

A Tough Mudder
for Tough Mothers

§

SEPTEMBER 4, 2012

OUR VACATION could have started better. After hours of our toddler daughter vomiting in the airport hotel, a deafening siren sounded at 2:00 A.M. and then continued to blare, interspersed with: "We have a reported emergency. Please stand by for further instructions."

No further instructions ever came, and my four-year-old son asked a remarkably astute question: "If it's an emergency, why aren't we leaving?" We imagined every terrifying scenario—while our daughter continued to vomit. At around 3:00 A.M. the alarm ceased, and we heard: "This was a system malfunction. We apologize for any inconvenience." This beginning was a harbinger of things to come, and we soon realized we'd gone about our trip preparation all wrong. Traveling cross-country with two small children—through four airports and on three flights, lasting twelve hours in one direction and twenty-six in the other—is decidedly not a vacation. It is more akin to running a Tough Mudder, without the glory.

Started by former British counter-terrorism agent Will Dean, Tough Mudders grew out of his "frustration with unimaginative and repetitive marathons, triathlons, mud runs, and other adventure runs," according to the Tough Mudder website. These ten- to twelve-mile events—designed to be mentally, physically, and emotionally challenging—include such daunting obstacles as fire walking, swimming in near-freezing water, and sprinting through a field of live wires.[3*]

Like an athlete preparing for a Tough Mudder, I must mentally prepare myself to fly. I used to refer to myself as a "white-knuckle flyer" because of my acute fear, but I'm really a "bare-knuckle flyer": I beat my fear into submission in order to get on a plane. My fear is based on close experience. My maternal grandfather, John J. Couchman, a talented gauge inspector at the Watervliet Arsenal near Albany, New York, was killed in a plane crash in March of 1972—only a few miles from his home. Oft-repeated statistics about how it is much safer to fly than to drive don't help soothe my flying anxiety. In my mind, his early death moved plane crashes from merely theoretical to horrifyingly real, so logic alone just doesn't help get me on the jet.

Instead, I gear up and prepare for battle. My poor spouse endures my plane-crash nightmares in the weeks leading up

---

[3*] As a distance runner myself, I take issue with Dean's dismissal of the challenge of a "monotonous" marathon. Frankly, it is a bit of a wimp-out that Mudder runners don't have to deal with the marathoners' tedium of mile after relentless mile—all the while knowing they're not actually going to win the race. But Tough Mudder races are designed to be a different kind of challenge than marathons and take plenty of grit to complete in their own right.

to any trip; once we're aboard she must bear with my disquiet over every patch of turbulence or unexpected noise. On this particular trip, my daughter's preflight sickness and the freaky emergency alarm did not aid my poor nerves. I just wasn't adequately prepared to test my strength, stamina, and mental grit.

My next mistake was in thinking that flying is still the glamorous and thrilling activity it used to be in, say, 1950, when only 17 million travelers passed through American airports. Many of today's 650 million passengers (who shuffle along wearing flip-flops and clothes that look suspiciously like their pajamas) are inevitably in my way on the moving walkways while I sprint—with kids in tow—to make an insanely tight connection to a horrifying small prop plane at the opposite end of the concourse. As a runner, I knew I could sprint to make connections. But I didn't factor in that my dashing and weaving—around stationary travelers on moving walkways— would necessarily involve hauling all the parenthood accoutrements. (My sincerest apologies to that poor guy in Denver whom I whacked with a diaper-stuffed tote bag.)

Although a Tough Mudder's challenges are daunting, they are entirely expected and prepared for. Not so the trials on our trip. I did not expect the broken plane, the missed connections, or the extra night in Denver. Nor did I anticipate the excessive turbulence on the hopper from Wyoming to Colorado—or my stomach's acute response to it. My lost purse, our missing baggage, the hour-long wait to rebook our flights, and the airport shuttle that simply wouldn't come were all additional, excruciating obstacles. But I also did not expect the revitalizing camaraderie I discovered along the way.

Here we are, a nation divided. Political parties and super PACs spend gobs of cash convincing us to hate one another. And yet. A stranger saw my anguish over my lost purse and ran alongside me through the Denver Airport to help me find the plane that was about to leave with my bag still on it. And yet. A gate agent marched out onto the tarmac and literally knocked on airplane doors to retrieve my purse. And yet. A minimum-wage food-service worker—without being asked—calculated the optimal use of my food vouchers to make sure that I'd have enough food for my kids in case we got stranded again.

Our family's Mudder did everything that the actual events promise. We tested our limits, and we learned the strength of our team. But more importantly than "unlocking a true sense of accomplishment," as advertised by Will Dean, I emerged from my trip with an unforeseen kinship with my fellow countrymen.

This affinity is what will enable me to get on the plane again next time so that my children can spend time with their grandparents. I know my own grandpa would have liked that.

Asking Favors

§

JULY 9, 2013

I ASKED THE TEACHER for a favor on the worst day possible. Monday dawns and each educator feels less like Plato and more like Sisyphus gazing wearily up a gargantuan hill. I knew this, and yet I still made my request in a crack-of-dawn e-mail: "Can you possibly write a letter of recommendation for me? Today? I need to send it off tonight."

I knew it was an unreasonable request, and I hated to even ask it. It revealed both my vulnerability and my utter dependence on her good will. I forced myself to do it, though, because I really wanted her recommendation, and I knew that the act would stretch me. But I didn't even consider that my appreciation of her willingness to comply with my urgent request would be rivaled by her own gratitude at having been asked.

After she'd completed my letter and I'd sent off my application, she confided that her initial thought had been: *How can she ask this of me on a Monday?!* But by successfully completing the letter, she'd learned a lot about herself. My asking her to do something that she initially thought Herculean gave her renewed confidence in her abilities. Her letter was a gratifying experience for each of us: I was admitted to the program I needed the letter for—the Campaign School at Yale—and I went on to have a fantastic educational experience, and she told me that she wrote one of the best recommendations of her life—under the gun, on a Monday. She realized in a new way that she really is a good writer and a truly loyal friend. Such a humble and yet daring act—on both our parts—took on much grander meaning.

It is difficult for many of us to ask for help; we often fear that our requests will be denied. Frank Flynn, associate professor of organizational behavior at the Stanford Graduate School of Business, and Jessica McCrory Calarco, assistant professor of sociology at Indiana University, jointly published a 2008 paper revealing that people tend to grossly underestimate how likely others are to agree to requests of assistance. In one of their studies, participants sought help from strangers by asking to borrow a cellphone or seeking complicated directions that required the strangers to walk them partway to their destination. Participants consistently overestimated by an average of 50 percent the number of strangers they would have to ask to get a certain number to agree to help. As Flynn recalled, "But they'd bound back to the lab afterwards with big smiles, saying, 'I can't believe how nice people were!'" Calarco and Flynn assert that this phenomenon of underestimation of others' altruism has to do with our inability to "get in the mind of the one being asked for help." There are strong feelings of social obligation at play, and people generally want to do the socially correct thing and give assistance.

Sometimes our reluctance to ask for help is masked by our own drive for self-sufficiency. Many of us in Vermont pride ourselves on our DIY (Do It Yourself) mentality and gumption. And let's face it, many of us are—in the words of my dad—"just cheap." I prefer to say "thrifty," but I am starting to understand his way of thinking. Several years ago, my wife and I planned to insulate our attic ourselves. After trying to load the surprisingly heavy insulation blower into the back of my aging Volvo, and realizing—as I saw the exceedingly patient worker at Leader Home Center raise his eyebrows— that I really had no clue as to how I would wrestle it out on the other end, I had to admit defeat. But, frankly, I was happy to do so. Paying the local professionals to insulate our attic was some of the best money I ever spent. I don't want to be cheap with my money, but more importantly I don't want to be stingy with my confidence in the superior skills and experience of others.

So, when we wanted to install a brick patio, my first thought was to hire a professional. But the man who'd been highly recommended to us couldn't fit us into his schedule. Feeling discouraged, I was about to say goodbye, but he told me to hang on and he'd walk me through the entire process, step by step. I wasn't prepared for this, so I furiously scribbled notes on a tiny scrap of paper entirely unsuited to the purpose. Fifteen minutes into his extremely detailed directions, I started to get antsy: *How am I going to wrap up this conversation?* But as I heard the pride in his voice as he shared his knowledge, it dawned on me that each of us was offering the other a gift. He felt bad that he couldn't squeeze me in to his busy schedule, but imparting his knowledge helped him feel useful and connected. And it gave me the confidence to complete the project while seeking the necessary help along the way. The herringbone brick patio that we built with his detailed instructions is gorgeous—a wonderful testament to a favor generously granted and willingly accepted.

One day, the same friend who'd written the letter of reference for me asked—on similarly short notice—if I would write one for her. I loved the symmetry of it all and the seeming ease with which she asked the favor.

The more we ask for help, the easier it becomes to see the strength in our vulnerability.

Stigma's Wrath

§

WHEN I FIRST HEARD of the unexpected death of popular Vermont Law School professor Cheryl Hanna, the pieces just didn't fit. She was forty-eight, healthy, and she died at home. There was that remote chance that she had had a sudden brain aneurysm or heart attack, but my intuition told me she'd taken her own life. When her husband told reporters that she'd been struggling through a severe bout of depression recently, the truth came into focus. My heart has been heavy for days.

My spouse and several of my close friends attended Vermont Law School where Hanna taught, one of the many jobs she juggled: commentator and contributor on both WCAX and VPR, lawyer, writer, mentor, and mom. I'd met Hanna, sat in on her class a few times, and even appeared in a short video that some friends produced for an assignment for her class. Hanna liked to keep things fun and interesting and was not above showing scenes from *My Cousin Vinnie* to demonstrate how to qualify an expert witness. As so many who knew her mourn her death, even more—including those who never met her—wonder why it had to come to this. Her close friend Ellen Sklar told a reporter, "She was more full of life than anyone I've ever known." And yet Hanna's husband, Paul Henninge, explained that Hanna "went to a dark place so quickly. For Cheryl, she began to loop. And when you loop in a dark place, you lose your ability to see outside of this dark place."

I am in my own loop—perseverating over what might have helped her let in some light. She was a very talented woman, a popular teacher, and someone with the means to get help. She also had so very much to live for; she left behind her eleven-year-old daughter and eight-year-old son. The thought that terrifies me is this: If depression can swallow her whole—someone with so many gifts and resources—how is *anyone* safe from its ravages? She hid her inner turmoil so well from her students, her colleagues, and her public. Henninge described Hanna's facility with concealment: "When she had her public face, she put on the face she wanted the public to see." How many people in your life—friends, family, neighbors, colleagues—do this same thing? Perhaps you yourself are among the one-in-four Vermonters doing this exhausting dance with mental illness and trying to "pass" because the public can seem so very unforgiving.

We have got to start talking more honestly about mental illness. Now. For those who have not suffered it, that kind of anguish is almost unfathomable. In quiet moments this week I have cried for Hanna, for her husband and her children. I can't help but wonder if the stigma of mental illness was a barrier to true healing for Hanna. Her husband said she did seek treatment in the past few months, but it seems clear she felt limited as a well-known public figure in Vermont's legal world and media. We live in such a small state where everyone knows each other and the gossip mill is fast and furious. Where could she turn and feel safe in anonymity?

The other night, while mulling over the horrible news about Cheryl Hanna, I unexpectedly picked up an interview with award-winning actress Glenn Close done by Jian Ghomeshi on *The Best of Q*, a program on CBC Radio. Close held me in rapt attention as she discussed how and why she speaks out against the societal stigma of mental illness. She shared with Ghomeshi her own family's experience with mental illness and addiction, and explained that she saw an important role for herself in changing the conversation. She says of her anti-stigma campaign, Bring Change 2 Mind, "I thought as a public figure I can help focus on the issue." Close continued, "Because everybody has been so reluctant, ashamed, fearful about talking about it openly, there has been no conversation. . . . If we talk about it enough, it will become natural." Mental illness is part of the human experience—and it occurs much too frequently to be called an anomaly. Close donated her time and talent to narrate a free, downloadable documentary, *A New State of Mind: Ending the Stigma of Mental Illness*, created by KVIE, Sacramento's public television station.

What struck me as I listened to her talk about her work was this: if even open, groovy California can't talk about this stuff, then surely we are doomed here in the taciturn, reserved Northeast. But the Brattleboro Retreat's "Stand up to Stigma" campaign is a strong start. We can all do much better in talking about mental illness. What might have happened if Hanna had felt able to talk openly and honestly about her struggles? What if she hadn't felt some obligation to be "perfect" for her colleagues, students, friends, and family? I'm certain that her circle of support did everything they could to help—as much as she would give them admission to her hell.

We all need to accept that highly accomplished, loving, lovely, and powerfully intelligent people can still be cripplingly depressed. We should also accept that, with proper treatment, they can continue to be highly accomplished, loving, lovely, and powerfully intelligent. But without sufficient treatment, this disease kills as surely as diabetes or heart disease.

Enough. Please start these important conversations. Secrets and euphemisms don't provide lasting hope for the future, just temporary and ephemeral refuge. And they contribute to taking gifted people from us.

The Girl in the Yellow Pantsuit

§

March 19, 2013

SEPTEMBER 1974: The pantsuit was canary yellow with appliqué patches on the chest and upper arms; it looked like a garage mechanic's coveralls. My mom purchased the outfit at Sears in anticipation of my first day of first grade. I loved that pantsuit, everything about it—the patches, the zipper, the collar, the bold yellow hue, and the fact that it was decidedly not a skirt or a dress. Despite being displayed in the girls' department, it had a certain boyish flair that appealed to the tomboy in me.

Like a driver holding back a purring machine, I was excited, elated, eager. I couldn't wait to get to school; I was ready to share my sheer awesomeness with my classmates.

I remember few details from that day except being teased so mercilessly that I vowed I'd never wear the pantsuit to school again. I desperately wanted my mom to take me home or bring me different clothes. I'm not certain what actually transpired. What I do remember—in fact, what I still feel in the pit of my stomach, now, almost forty years later—is shame.

What exactly did I have to feel ashamed about? Certainly it's not comfortable or pleasant to be mocked for one's snazzy, albeit unconventional and poorly received outfit. But my bright yellow pantsuit—not unlike a neon light flashing its truth—tapped into something I was already wrestling with at the age of six: the despair that comes from realizing that you are out of sync. There's a code, a rhythm of life, and you don't know it. I was ashamed that I'd so boldly put myself forward in an audacious zipper jumper that proclaimed my difference. I've been unraveling that shame for decades.

Turns out, I am not alone. Dr. Brené Brown—a research professor at the University of Houston Graduate School of Social Work and TED Talk phenom—has spent her career studying shame, vulnerability, and courage. When she filmed her initial TED Talk on vulnerability, she felt so exposed afterwards that she didn't leave her house for days. Her embarrassment over her own personal reaction to her research was crushing; she felt ill when she considered that hundreds of people in the audience had witnessed her raw honesty and authenticity.

In the midst of her self-described "breakdown" (although her therapist insists that it was "a spiritual awakening"), she couldn't conceive that her research would resonate so deeply with others and that her talk, "The Power of Vulnerability," would soon be watched by millions.[4*] It is mesmerizing to watch this funny, whip-smart Texan, who is so very

---

[4*] Originally broadcast locally in the Houston area, the video of this TED Talk has now been viewed 54 million times.

uncomfortable with her own vulnerability, stand up on stage and wrestle with it.

In thousands of interviews and stories collected over six years, Brown noticed an unexpected and discomfiting paradox: our shame is rooted in the very same thing that will release us from it—vulnerability. Brown defines *shame* as a fear of disconnection. We ask ourselves, "Is there something about me that, if others knew it, it would cause them to reject me?" This fear of rejection is the very thing that keeps people from having true connection. And it is those who fully embrace vulnerability—who believe that their imperfections actually make them beautiful and worthy—who live best with courage and compassion. Brown asserts that vulnerability is the birthplace of joy, creativity, belonging, and love; it is absolutely fundamental to use it to overcome our shame.

The vulnerability that Brown discusses in her books and in her talks, although it is something we often recoil from in our own lives, is what we unconsciously look for in others. We identify it not as weakness but as courage and an underlying confidence. It goes beyond the hackneyed phrase "He's man enough to cry." It's about having the self-assurance to show your humanity—complete with your untidy inadequacies and shortcomings. We are drawn to those who are wholehearted, and we see their vulnerability as strength, not weakness.

That's why I found President George W. Bush's comments after the September 11 horror so very disappointing. When the nation's heart had been torn open, and while we fought to staunch the flow, the president reassured us that "America is open for business." Yes, he was facing enormous economic pressures, and he certainly felt an obligation to claim that he

would keep us safe from further harm. But his unwillingness to be vulnerable made me feel less safe. His posturing
looked childish. He didn't have the strength or confidence to
acknowledge his own despair and to trust that we, as a grieving nation, could take it.

I recently spoke to a young machinist at a manufacturing
plant in Maine who sheepishly admitted that he had never
finished high school, that he had only just completed his
GED. The look on his face said so much: shame, embarrassment, hope that I'd understand, and a desire to be respected
anyway. His bravery in exposing himself was startling and,
yes, surprisingly charming. Witnessing him face his shame—
and then hold it out for inspection—moved me to consider
my own vulnerability.

For years I thought no one would ever find me attractive. It
was like I existed as that six-year-old in the yellow pantsuit—
always out of step. Not good enough. Now I'm returning to
something I knew back before my shame and disappointment
took hold. We should be audacious, daring, and vulnerable.
Sharing one's whole self, bright yellow pantsuit and all—
draws others to you.

When Failure is a Gift

§

MANY COACHES, therapists, and mentors pose a question to get their clients to open up, dream bigger, and stretch themselves: What would you do if you couldn't fail? It's intended to point people in the direction of their true passions—to encourage us to live our lives "all the way up" because (although we don't want to admit it) we all have limited time. I've asked friends and colleagues this same question, too, and it has sometimes helped to shake something loose within the person and move them closer to fulfillment. But recently I've been pondering another probing question: What will you do when you do fail?

As I approached what I call my Great Awakening—though my spouse might call it a midlife crisis—I took up all the hobbies I'd always wanted to pursue, like jazz vocals, illustrating, and trumpet lessons. I also wanted a motorcycle. In my motorcycle training course, I was by far the oldest and the tiniest student, and one of only two women. I was also the only person in the course who failed the final practicum. I dropped the bike on a sharp U-turn, which is an automatic fail—as it should be. Riding a fast hunk of metal is obviously quite dangerous; you need to have the skills to navigate potential hazards.

But knowing that this automatic fail was solely for my own safety didn't help in the moment. I still felt disappointed in myself and very embarrassed. I was also really frustrated. And I absolutely did not want to cry as I left the test site. So I just nodded, squinted hard so my hot tears wouldn't slip out, and pursed my lips as the instructor told me that I should still stick around until after the others' tests were done. I sat in our very uncool minivan and cried; I raged at myself for failing.

It took several weeks before I could think about next steps. I couldn't imagine getting back on a motorcycle, not because I was scared but because the bike would remind me that I'd failed—that I'd tried so hard, and I'd still failed.

But slowly—over several weeks—I eventually plotted how I would make my own proving ground at the high school parking lot. I'd get chalk, cones, and a measuring tape. And I'd just practice over and over again until I mastered it.

Which is exactly what I did, day after day during the hottest part of that summer. Sometimes my young daughter would ride her bike out there with me. I'd go through my makeshift course, and she'd make a video, complete with commentary, so I could look at my successes and mistakes. And then she'd do the course on her little bicycle, which was—as you can imagine—completely adorable.

When I rode up to Springfield to take my road test again, it was a damp, cold, miserable October day. But as I traveled the slick back roads in the early morning light, I realized that I'd shed my embarrassment and frustration. It also dawned on me that I was glad I'd failed the first time. The experience pushed me to truly nail down critical skills and helped me rediscover parts of myself I really like: my grit and tenacity.

The best part, even a year later, has been randomly running into folks from my motorcycle class. Each time it's the same: "Did you stick with it? Did you pass? Are you riding?" As I grin and shake my head yes, the hand goes up for the high five. I feel as if I keep succeeding over and over again. It's a wonderful feeling.

Navigating Slippery Conversations

§

NOVEMBER 21, 2019

T HERE'S A STEEP, ROCKY TRAIL on one of my morning hikes that's now covered with wet oak leaves. I recently trudged up the slope as two walkers slip-slided down. Confident hikers all, we marveled that we can still lose our footing on these greasy autumn offerings. That's how we sometimes feel when navigating social situations in which a colleague, a friend, a family member, or a stranger says something offensive; we often lose our confidence and stumble.

I was reminded of the seasonal slick carpet of autumn oak leaves while facilitating a breakout session at the annual Vermont Vision for a Multicultural Future conference. In this dynamic two-day event, participants themselves create the agenda for the conference and then facilitate all the workshops. This is not a space in which you can sit back and be a passive participant. You must walk on the oak leaves.

I've attended this conference in the past, but this year I facilitated the breakout session of all the White people attending the conference. In an adjacent room, Curtiss Reed facilitated a session for People of Color.

These topics—racial justice, racism, and White supremacy—are so complex and so fraught with intense emotions that sometimes those of us who want to have meaningful, substantive conversations feel paralyzed and don't speak about what's genuinely on our minds or in our hearts. For People of Color, there is the exhaustion and frustration that comes from constantly having to educate others about these issues. People of Color also face real danger when they speak up.

Meanwhile, some White people deny that there's a problem. Others understand that racism is real but don't want to believe that it's systemic or institutional. As Toni Morrison wrote in the 2016 essay "Mourning for Whiteness: "So scary are the consequences of a collapse of White privilege that many Americans have flocked to a political platform that supports and translates violence against the defenseless as strength. These people are not so much angry as terrified, with the kind of terror that makes knees tremble."

And then there are White people who truly want to be strong allies but don't always find the courage or the right words. Sometimes it's about finding a good moment to inter-ject, or using the right tone. And sometimes power comes into play. What do you do when it's a boss or supervisor who makes an offensive remark? I know these issues are real and can be impediments to showing up as strong allies. The par-ticipants in the workshop for White people were honest and open with one another and wanted help figuring out how to navigate these conversations.

Here's a way to begin to be a better ally when an opportunity to speak up arises. Start with a clarifying question: Why do you feel that way? Or: I don't understand; what did you mean by that? Curiosity gives someone the opportunity to reflect on what they said and why. Questions create an opening for a more substantive conversation.

When others are around, sometimes what's called for is a clear signal to the rest of the group: "I'm not sure what you meant by that comment, but here's what I heard." Or "I don't think you meant to offend, but here's why that comment is hurtful." There might be situations in which there's no time to stop for clarifying questions. You can show your unease or displeasure through facial expressions and body language, and then follow up with the person afterwards.

We have inherited a path covered in slippery oak leaves. But if we navigate that path together, with curiosity, humility, and tenacity, we create the possibility that the people coming behind us will have slightly less treacherous footing.

Expanding the Story

§

ONCE, after witnessing an epic meltdown of a child in a grocery store, an acquaintance said, "I'm sure *your* kids are well behaved. You and Elizabeth are excellent parents." I felt instantly uncomfortable and replied, "You never know what families struggle with. I doubt that kid's behavior has much to do with that woman's parenting." She gave me a doubtful look that said, "Yeah, right," and we moved on to another topic. But the conversation gave me a knot in my stomach whenever I thought about it.

This incident occurred years before my son's autism spectrum diagnosis. But even before I had a name for it, I knew there were aspects of his behavior that had little to do with our parenting. We couldn't work any harder. And we were exhausted and discouraged a lot of the time. All our love, support, and effort didn't change the fact that navigating the world was really difficult and bewildering for him.

Our son talked early and had an uncanny facility with language. His vocabulary, at age five, was already sprinkled with words like *oscillating* and *precipice*. Our conversations routinely astonished eavesdroppers. I got used to the question "How old is that kid?"

But early on—when he was around the age of four–there were signs that his experience of the world was quite different from ours. If we got caught in a sudden downpour, he'd shriek in discomfort. He hated the feeling of wet clothes on his skin. Particular smells and sounds drove him to distraction. We once left a preschool field trip because the store attached to the sugarhouse had strong smells. He took one sniff and moaned, "No, Mom! I want to go," as he pulled me out the door.

Changes in routine, even slight, would send him into a terrified panic. When we went to the playground and someone was on the swing he'd used the last time, he'd be utterly inconsolable. It was not a tantrum; it was well beyond a tantrum. It was a little guy screaming out that the world made no sense to him. And it was painful, most of all, to realize that my attentiveness and tenderness didn't automatically help him make sense of the world—or allow others to see beyond his behavior to his burgeoning creativity and adoration of infants.

If you're a parent of a child who is neurodiverse, you know what I'm talking about. It's lonely. Our son guilelessly recounted conversations he'd had with various adults at school when he'd had a difficult day navigating social cues that he didn't understand. He'd say: "Mrs. So and So said the reason I'm a sore loser is because you haven't taught me how to be a good sport. Is that true?" I had to practice keeping my face slack so he couldn't read my fury and despair when he reported such incidents to us.

What has saved me from permanent sorrow for the past seven years has been our friends who also have complicated kids—those kids for whom making eye contact is incredibly unsettling and uncomfortable. The kids who have to work so very hard to filter out sensory input and can't quite act "appropriately" in a crowd. The kids who receive a steady stream of judgment from onlookers but whose daily triumphs—sitting through a sibling's dance performance without completely losing it—often go unremarked upon.

Compassion and patience do not come naturally to my son, but he understands storytelling. When we share ideas together at dinner time, he will often chime in with "Tell me a long, detailed story about that." He then grabs onto interesting, funny tidbits and digs deeper into the complexities and layers of the story. Together, the family will swing out into a half-dozen mini-stories before returning once again to the central story. We often generate more questions and details, and we'll scramble to look up a date, a person in history or perhaps a definition. The stories lead to more stories, creating a wonderful loop of curiosity. Through this process we are working to teach him that the stories we tell about one another are almost always incomplete. Making room for another narrative nudges us all towards our better selves. That's what I hope for all of us in the New Year.

Reaching Out with the Great Power of Empathy

§

ONE DAY LAST YEAR, as I was dropping off my kids at school, I noticed a parent and child who were really struggling. The girl screamed and threw her backpack at a car and then sat on the little stone wall crying. The mom seemed near tears as well.

I slid out of my car and called out, "Your girl's having a hard morning, isn't she? I understand. Our mornings are often like that, too." I reminded her of who my kids were and then said, "You're doing such a good job. It's really, really hard, I know. But you're a good mom; you're a really good mom."

And then I asked if she wanted a hug, and I wrapped my arms around her. And she cried. I didn't try to fix her problem or offer advice. I didn't brainstorm solutions or ask her to tell me about her morning. I just acknowledged what I'd seen, validating her struggle. We don't do this enough—just sitting with sadness and discomfort, letting another human being know we see her pain and we care. Not judging, not problem-solving—just listening and holding emotion.

Dr. Brené Brown, a researcher at the University of Houston, says fundamental research on judgment shows that "we only judge in areas where we're the most susceptible to shame. So we only judge and put value on people's behaviors in areas where we believe sometimes we're not enough, which is why things like parenting are judgment minefields—because every single one of us who's doing it knows we're screwing it up every day."

I've written here for over six years and published hundreds of columns. People routinely stop me on the street to talk about my writing and what it has meant for them. I've grown accustomed to the public exchange of ideas and emotions. But nothing prepared me for the response I received from last week's column on parenting my child who's on the autism spectrum. E-mails, texts, and Facebook messages and posts have poured in. People have stopped me in the grocery store and in the coffee shop to talk, often in hushed tones, about what it meant for them to have their experience validated. They shared thanks and great relief; they spoke of heartache and anger. They also expressed a weary loneliness. But they often shared hope, too—one parent to another—that things will get easier.

Underpinning all of it, I believe, is the fact that people desperately want to be seen. And something profound happens when a writer shines a light on sorrowful, desolate places. The illumination is healing; there's connection where before there was isolation. And seeing our own experiences in someone else's writing frees us to let go—to release an emotional knot we've worried over for too long.

What parents overwhelmingly conveyed to me, in response to my column last week, was that they just want more empathy. Whether it's from neighbors, strangers, teachers, or extended family, they simply want people to be more empathetic and less judgmental. This does not seem like a big ask. But, as Dr. Brown would remind us, that means first judging ourselves less—letting go of our own shame. Sometimes the best assistance we can offer others is simply to acknowledge them, to sit with them in sorrow or grief or despair without needing to fix or judge.

I'm so fortunate to have a platform from which I can call people towards a better way of being in community with one another. In writing last week's column, in sharing my own heartache and struggles, I wanted to give others permission to be more gentle with themselves and a little more candid with others.

Part Four

§

Hope

A Walk in the Woods

§

APRIL 11, 2019

I HAVE ALWAYS BEEN PRONE to worry. In my legislative life, I fret about bills, vote counts, and how my constituents are going to make ends meet. It's not easy to quiet my brain; there's so much important work to be done. And although I've heard throughout my whole adult life that meditation could help settle my hyperactive mind, it doesn't seem to work for me. Quiet moments of simply sitting and breathing often turn into long minutes of list-making in my head: calls, e-mails, and texts I need to return. Although in my less forgiving moments I call this perseverating, at other times I know that this hypervigilance serves me and pushes me to work hard. But, of course, I still need peaceful time to recharge. And I find that solace in the woods.

My young daughter, Sarah, has recently started to join me on my weekend jaunts. Several weeks ago I returned home from a long romp in the woods with the wing of a barred owl I'd found on the trail, clearly the result of an attack by a

129

predator. When I showed it to Sarah and demonstrated how the wing folded up like fan, she was beyond entranced. The look on her face was identical to the one she got this winter when we were out cross-country skiing and found an animal skull. It is a look of pure bliss and wonder. Finding these treasures is more glorious to her than finding a wad of cash. She feels like she's been let in on a special secret.

Last summer, she attended one of the day camps run by the Vermont Wilderness School (VWS), and she found her people. Whittling, tracking animals, building fires, and simply reveling in the woods put her in touch with a core part of her identity. This wasn't news to us; as a very young girl, she thought worms and crickets were the most amazing beings on the planet. And she'd call her wary brother over to see "the most adorable slugs ever!"

She now does the VWS school-year program called Great Blue Heron. Every Wednesday she spends the day in the woods of Marlboro and then emerges from the forest covered in dirt, charcoal, and brambles. There's always a grin on her face and an air of both confidence and self-satisfaction. Her brother is intrigued by her identity as woodswoman, but there is no envy. He recently said to me on the drive to pick her up, "Can you think of anything more distasteful than spending the entire day in the woods?" Abe prefers a good hotel with a pool and room service.

Last weekend in the woods, Sarah and I brought along a canvas bag filled with sketchbooks and pencils so that she could stop alongside streams and rock formations when inspiration struck. In the end, she decided not to do any sketching; she wanted to do a long hike instead. By the end of our adventure, we'd collected feathers, glittering rocks, interesting sticks, and other wondrous things from along the Retreat Trails. She remarked that it had been a "perfect" morning, and I heartily agreed.

When we'd first headed into the woods that day, my heart was heavy and my mind was feeling dark. I felt ill-equipped to do my work and could feel self-doubt taking charge of my inner dialogue. I was dreading facing my chock-full legislative e-mail inbox.

Several hours later, we both felt completely rejuvenated—a glorious mix of calm and energy. I was ready to do the hard work ahead.

Craving a Different Kind of Leadership

§

July 26, 2019

I T's EASY TO FEEL despondent about the news: the humanitarian crisis at the southern United States border; the revelation that Purdue Pharma knew, years ago, how addictive its opioid pharmaceuticals were; and the recent speech by President Trump in which he asserted that Article II of the US Constitution gives him the right to do whatever he wants. It feels as if the world is fraying at the edges, and it's difficult to find examples of the courageous leadership I crave. I want to see leadership that's grounded in authenticity and uses transparency and vulnerability as powerful means of connection.

After I left a career in teaching and before I entered politics, I trained as a coach through CTI—the Coaches Training Institute—and coached individuals and groups to help them achieve personal and professional fulfillment. I had to get over the decidedly "California" flavor of the work and my own

New England bias about that. But once I did, I fully embraced the way that so-called co-active coaching can transform lives and relationships. Although my extremely busy schedule does not allow me to coach individual clients anymore, I have used my training to design workshops and trainings on cultivating authentic leadership within individuals and groups. I recently ran a two-hour workshop for a department within state government; I left feeling hopeful and excited.

In my workshops and trainings, I start from this place of introduction: "I am both talented and flawed." The participants must understand from our very first moments together that I will show them my vulnerability. I can't ask them to be authentic if I'm not willing to do that myself. To say that I am flawed is really just an open acknowledgment of something we all already know. But when we can name it and start from the fundamental truth that we all have talents and flaws, opportunities open up for authentic leadership. Real connection and trust can be built upon that base.

The era of the bullheaded, claptrap-spewing, paternalistic bossman is waning. I know it doesn't look that way, given what we see in the Oval Office, but it's on the way out. Trump's style is not the leadership of the future; it's dated, stagnant, and infantile. And it's not what most people want. But they must be offered an alternative. That starts with owning our gifts and our weaknesses.

I often hear people say, "I just want to have an impact." What they really mean is: "I want to have a lasting, positive impact." Greater impact begins with naming and owning the impact we're already having. Every single day, we have hundreds of opportunities for impact—moments in which we affect the people around us. How did you treat the bagger who helped you with your groceries? What did you say to the employee who came to ask you for help? What did your body language and your tone of voice signal when you entered your most recent work meeting?

Trust and good leadership are built in many small moments—not usually from grand gestures. Unintended impact—positive and negative—happens constantly. When we become more aware of this and use those moments to show leadership and vulnerability, we can have a positive daily impact on those around us. And those small moments of trust between individuals builds a stronger team that, collectively, has a greater positive impact.

Several constituents have said to me recently that they just don't know what to do in order to feel better about the state of the world. My advice to them is simple: Start small and create moments of positive impact with the next person you encounter. It will help to sustain you in these deeply disturbing times, and that feeling of connection will enable you to be a better leader.

Climate Conversations

§

L IKE SO MANY VERMONTERS, I'm concerned about how a heating planet will impact the most vulnerable throughout our state, across the nation, and around the world. And I sometimes feel paralyzed by the enormity of the problem. I've searched for another way for us to talk about climate change without feeling despondent. This is a huge challenge for all of us who care about the environment and climate action: How do we pivot towards hope? Atmospheric scientist Dr. Katharine Hayhoe may have the answer.

Hayhoe is a highly esteemed Canadian climate scientist who also happens to be an evangelical Christian living in West Texas. I can easily imagine a comedy sketch on Saturday Night Live poking fun at a right-wing Christian climate scientist in the middle of oil country who tilts at metaphorical windmills. The incongruous mashup of seemingly contradictory identities is not lost on Hayhoe. She understands the great challenge of her work: convincing those on the right, including many evangelicals, that climate change is both real and man-made. I'm greatly inspired by Hayhoe and her work.

You may have first heard of Hayhoe in 2012, when Newt Gingrich asked her to write a chapter for a book he was editing on the environment. He assumed that because she was an evangelical that she would deny climate science. When she asserted that climate change was not a liberal hoax, he removed the chapter from the book.

But Hayhoe didn't retreat. She sought out fellow conservatives to discuss the complex subject of climate change and realized that people who doubt climate change—or don't feel compelled to act—won't change with more facts. The "fact deluge" method falsely assumes that people are simply blank slates just waiting to be written on with more correct information. But we're not blank slates; we already have a strong set of beliefs, often tied to our identity. And when people challenge that identity, we usually feel attacked. And when we feel attacked, it's very hard for us to listen. We instead protect ourselves. We don't generally want to roll up our sleeves to get to work. Hiding under a blanket seems preferable.

Hayhoe figured out that more-hopeful conversations and genuine personal connection will work to change hearts and minds on the topic of climate change. She has spent years tailoring her talks on climate change to her specific audiences. Hayhoe starts from a place of connection. What do we have in common? What values do we share? And then she connects through those values in order to build common purpose and generate movement in a positive direction. She does not start with "Here is why you need to care about climate change"; rather, she seeks to understand what her audience cares about.

What have they noticed in their own lives? Does there seem to be less snow on the ski slopes? Are they now spending less money on heating fuel but more on electric bills from their air-conditioning? Is the prevalence of childhood asthma on the rise in their area? Once people identify shared concerns, the connections to the larger issue of climate change can happen organically. While her strategy may not work on the cynical climate deniers—those who deny climate change for political gain rather than out of conviction—her method helps regular people connect on issues they care about.

As we do this work, we need to help each other pivot towards hope. We must channel our curiosity and our wonder and our belief that we can make positive change. And we should cultivate the feeling that moving us towards an energy-independent Vermont is exciting. For example, safeguarding our rivers and lakes for future generations is rooted in love for our children and our communities. And that expanding our weatherization programs is completely in line with our values as thrifty New Englanders.

I know that when we consider the terrible local flooding from Tropical Storm Irene, the horrific wildfires in California, the devastation from Hurricane Maria in Puerto Rico, or the catastrophic destruction caused by Superstorm Sandy, it can feel like we need to employ some magical thinking to believe that we can slow or reverse this frightening trend. But Hayhoe shows us another way to have these hard conversations, ground them in reality, and make real change. When we connect through our shared values with a vision of what we want in our own communities, it becomes easier to identify concrete actions we can take to work towards that vision. And action will generate hope.

Don't Hesitate

§

JANUARY 24, 2019

L AST WEEK, I attended a meeting in which Vermont House members and senators discussed legislative priorities for our work in fighting climate change. The subject is somber, but spirits were high as we shared ideas for bills and topics to be discussed. The sheer number of legislators in the room—and the ensuing jocular conversations—made my heart lighter, despite my deep concerns about climate change and its terrible toll.

As I sat amid the commotion, a text from a dear friend flashed on my phone. It read: "Mary Oliver died. I'm in my office crying. I knew you'd understand."

I did understand. Mary Oliver, the Pulitzer Prize–winning poet, wrote more than twenty volumes of verse, and I often sought solace in those volumes. Oliver has been likened to many greats: Walt Whitman, Emily Dickinson, and Robert Frost. And, as the *New York Times* writer Margalit Fox pointed out in her obituary of Oliver, she also had become something of a "bookish rock star" in her elderly years. Thousands of us cherish her attention to sublime details and her exhortations for us to truly see—and revel—in the natural world.

What she also offered to us was permission—glorious license, in fact—to feel at once joyful and sorrowful. Her celebration of moments, of tiny interactions and observations, were her pleas to allow ourselves to just be. To sit with heartbreaking loveliness and let ourselves be enchanted—even as we know that the moment will pass, and that we will pass.

In the days after Oliver died, I could feel a different urgency within me. It wasn't that everything now felt fleeting or ethereal—like a bud opening or a cricket springing. It was that everything at once seemed to matter more. My interactions with people felt more consequential. My work felt weightier. I was more attuned to the sound of squeaking snow under my footfalls, and I noticed the way the ice formed on the edges of the roof. I became fully aware that I was now fifty; it's likely that the bulk of my years have already been lived.

While I was clumsily carrying these plaintive thoughts and feelings, my family hatched a plan. We'd heard that the ice on Spofford Lake in Chesterfield, New Hampshire, had frozen in a spectacular way. The edges of the lake were cloudy, but the center of the lake was like black glass. We'd seen videos on social media of our friends skating on this remarkably smooth, clear ice. I'd been curious about it, but now I felt an obligation. It was a stunning gift offered to all of us, and it felt ungracious not to accept it. So we went to see the ice and rejoice.

As I gingerly walked out onto the center of the frozen lake, feeling awe and relief that we still have winter, I recalled

Oliver's poem "Don't Hesitate." She writes, "If you suddenly and unexpectedly feel joy, / don't hesitate. Give in to it." I watched my son run, dive, and slide on the miraculously clear ice as his sister leaped and turned on her skates.

My children's glee breathed new life into Oliver's words:

>... There are plenty
>of lives and whole towns destroyed or about
>to be. We are not wise, and not very often
>kind. And much can never be redeemed.
>Still, life has some possibility left. Perhaps this
>is its way of fighting back, that sometimes
>something happens better than all the riches
>or power in the world. It could be anything,
>but very likely you notice it in the instant
>when love begins. Anyway, that's often the
>case. Anyway, whatever it is, don't be afraid
>of its plenty. Joy is not made to be a crumb.

The Natural World as Spiritual Realm

§

OCTOBER 24, 2019

I N THE BOUGHS of our large spruce tree is a fairy house that my daughter built last year. At the base of the maple by our back door is another. They are reminders to me of many things: my fierce love for my daughter, the delight I feel in the unexpected, and the importance of slowing down. They're also signals to me that my sense of the spiritual resides in the natural world. It's why I try to get into the woods every day; whether I'm in Brattleboro or Montpelier, I need the solace, the calm, and the opportunity to center myself in spirituality. I know that many friends and neighbors feel the same way.

At a recent meeting of the Vermont Housing and Conservation Board (VHCB), a member stressed the strong connection many Vermonters feel between the natural world and spirituality. Our state may have the smallest percentage of residents who attend a house of worship—according to a 2015 Gallup poll, only 17 percent of Vermonters regularly attend religious services. But our low level of church attendance doesn't necessarily indicate any lack of spiritual connection; for many of us, the natural world is a manifestation of the divine—both awe-inspiring and a confirmation that we're part of something much larger than ourselves.

There's a growing body of research that suggests that more time spent in the natural world also improves health outcomes. Time in nature has been linked to stress relief and lower levels of anxiety and depression. Short-term memory also seems to be improved by exposure to nature. Another study suggests that spending time sleeping in the forest can lower levels of cortisol, a hormone linked to stress. And still other studies demonstrate that mood, focus, and self-esteem improve after exposure to the natural environment.

In fact, a relatively new body of research has also shown that interaction with the natural world can elicit a powerful emotional and psychological response: awe. In a landmark 2003 paper, psychologists Dacher Keltner—professor of psychology at the University of California, Berkeley—and Jonathan Haidt—professor of ethical leadership at New York University—presented a new conceptual approach to understanding awe. Keltner and Haidt suggested that the experience of awe forces us to react to a "perceived vastness" that we then "accommodate" in our worldview.

"Perceived vastness" can come from a variety of experiences—from viewing the Grand Canyon or the mighty trees of Yosemite to meeting a powerful person or contemplating complex ideas such as the infinitude of the universe. These experiences can shift our attention away from ourselves and towards others and the vastness of the world. This, in turn, can help us feel more generous towards others.

Keltner and Haidt assert that when we experience awe and subsequent self-transcendent emotions, we must change our thinking to accommodate these new feelings and thoughts. In short, awe is a powerful experience that can shift our understanding of the world. Studies appear to indicate that people who experience awe are less tied to "internal scripts," are more open to incorporate new information into their worldview, and are more likely to demonstrate greater humility in their interactions with others.

The Vermont woods offer endless invitations to experience awe. It could be the sweeping views from Camel's Hump or a salamander meandering over brilliant autumn leaves or even the tiny natural fairy dwellings that are produced at the Grafton Nature Museum's annual Fairy House Fest. All these moments present opportunities for me to connect with my sense of awe and my understanding of the divine. In turn, my feelings of awe help me reach outward to my community.

Quite simply, I'd be lost without my forest rambles.

Peak Moments

§

"Y OU'LL NEVER GET a meal cooked in this weather," the hiker remarked; he left no room for possibility. He then chided me: "You'll just have to resign yourselves to a cold dinner like the rest of us." The storm, now fully gathered, released heavy drops on my neck and back as I hunched over our dented Peak 1 backpacking stove. My charges—a gaggle of thirteen-year-old girls—looked hopeful and powerful with their bright, sweaty faces and their dirty, scratched-up legs. There was no way I was going to offer these gals a cold dinner after they'd just hauled their outsized backpacks up Shrewsbury Peak.

That stranger's implied challenge set me on a path that led through one of my biggest challenges but also became a peak experience, a time of being fully "in the flow." I felt completely engaged and alive in a new way. Yesterday's weather—the air's heaviness, mingled with the heady smell of pine needles—reminded me of this long-ago episode. The memory of that experience offers succor in times of doubt; it recalls the utter joy and satisfaction that can emerge from staring down adversity and prevailing.

Positive psychologist Abraham Maslow first developed the idea of "peak experiences" in his 1964 book *Religions, Values, and Peak Experiences*. Maslow asserts these peak human experiences are "moments of highest happiness and fulfillment" and are characterized by a sensation of being your whole and harmonious self. These are times when a person has the feeling of using all capacities and capabilities and being able to function effortlessly and easily. I am grateful to Maslow that I have words to put to the feelings of deep resonance I experienced in the Green Mountains twenty years ago.

It had been days of hard hiking in intense heat, followed by violent storms each night. By the time we trudged to the top of Shrewsbury Peak, we were ready for the shelter offered by the lean-to. But another group had already set up shop there, so we headed back into the forest to tie up our tarps. We needn't have bothered with our fancy knotwork and ingenious rigging. That night's storm was so relentless that rivulets ran right under the tarps and into our sleeping bags. As physically uncomfortable as I was, I knew the girls were emotionally tender—nervous about being out in the woods, thoroughly soaked, and accompanied by adults other than their parents.

Campfires can work miracles on weary spirits, so I understood the necessity of careful preparation and planning. I always hike with a Ziploc bag of materials—dry birch bark, bits of brittle hemlocks twigs, and other supplies critical to the purpose. But my tinder pouch was dangerously low after many nights of rain: it was time to rally the troops.

My intrepid campers gathered more hemlock twigs and wrist-sized branches from the forest floor. We stripped the wet bark off and uncovered the pale heartwood. We then carved off the damp outer layers and whittled shavings of dry bits. The girls protected the pile and then slipped it into a plastic bag for later. Next, we dug a fire pit and ringed it with rocks, close enough to the other group's shelter to use the roof's overhang to our advantage but not so close that we might burn the whole thing down. We constructed drying racks out of branches and cord we'd brought for emergencies.

One hour later, we wolfed down a hot meal and slipped into warm, dry sleeping bags. Single-minded, and working in unity, we'd achieved something we all thought was impossible.

And what of the hiker who'd started me off in "the flow" with his chiding? We shared our hot meal with him, of course.

Pink Light on the Snow

§

DECEMBER 27, 2019

FTER AN ESPECIALLY WINDY NIGHt last week, I noticed that powerful gusts had torn hundreds of tiny hemlock branches from larger limbs; they were now strewn before me on the snow. The twigs looked like the outstretched arms of hundreds of people reaching for one another but remaining separated—almost touching, but not quite. I couldn't think of much else on that morning hike except for the distance between outstretched arms.

There are some who benefit when people are divided. They seek political gain, economic advantage, or a kind of religious superiority. But the great mass of us get no tangible benefit from this partitioning. At times we unwittingly fall into our own small-scale version of this. A phenomenon that University of Texas professor Brené Brown calls "common enemy intimacy." It's when closeness is built by talking trash about other people. Brown explains the problem: "What we have is not real. The intimacy we have is built on hating the same people. And that's counterfeit. That's counterfeit trust. That's not real." And it will come as no surprise that this kind of false closeness doesn't actually bridge chasms; it creates more.

Many of us see the divisions that Trumpism has created and decry the divides that it has exacerbated. We understand that the president's hateful invectives sow division and discord. But it's more difficult to figure out what part we all play in this—especially if we don't support his abject chicanery or his wholesale rejection of truth or basic decency. Where do the majority of Americans fit into this tragedy? Are we blameless bystanders? Unwitting accomplices through our silence or inaction? Perhaps many are numb to the gross transgressions because to be aware is to be truly terrified.

I keep returning to the words of nineteenth-century British philosopher and political economist John Stuart Mill: "Bad men need nothing more to compass their ends, than that good men should look on and do nothing." I've exhorted my readers for years to find our strength and grit and use our voices to reject tyranny in its current form: populism sliding unapologetically towards fascism. But I've become keenly aware that fear not only contributes to our loneliness and collective grief, it also keeps us disconnected from each other and unfocused in our power.

We need to bridge the distance between those outstretched arms if we're to have any impact at all. This idea is not new. Anglo-Irish politician and philosopher Edmund Burke gave voice to this in the eighteenth century, but every generation seems to have to relearn it. Burke wrote, "When bad men combine, the good must associate; else they will fall one by one, an unpitied sacrifice in a contemptible struggle." Few of us want to be a sacrificial lamb, an offering to a despotic force. But most of us are made more courageous by the moments of valor we see in the lives of our friends and neighbors, in those times when we sense we're not alone.

Several days after my walk through the delicate hemlock sticks, I headed into the woods at dawn. The sun rose and cast long beams of soft pink light on the snow as it flashed through the tree branches. Where the light landed, the snow glowed, almost pulsing from the infusion of brightness and warmth. Inexplicably, I felt more hopeful about our ability to bridge the distance between one another. There are many mornings when I feel shrouded in darkness; these are such perilous times. But the pink light on the snow reminds me that deep courage is born in brief moments of bravery. May we all find moments of courage in the New Year.

A Sense of Wonder
to Balance Out the Anger

§

AUGUST 8, 2019

WHILE TRAIL RUNNING several weeks ago, I wondered if I'd see a turtle on my dawn romp. Minutes later, I rounded a curve in the trail, and there was a lovely painted turtle on the path. I stood and just beamed. Then I saw another turtle. And another. Then another. I was elated and also very confused. Then I realized that these splendid turtles were all laying eggs; I'd basically wandered into a turtle delivery ward. I gasped and felt utterly gleeful, and I carried that delight with me all week. It was a much-needed balm.

I hope I never lose that sense of wonder. There's so much darkness right now, so many horrible events to make me despair about this world; I need these moments of release. It's not because I'm embracing denial. Nor do I want to partake in the collective amnesia that the country seems to have within twenty-four hours after the president's most recent offensive tweet. It's not about turning away from the fight; it's about gearing up for the long haul.

A young man recently asked me how I stay positive when the news is so very dark. He sees the nasty culture wars raging around him and wants to be politically engaged, but he asked, "How do you sustain your energy and not get depressed?" It was an excellent question. I don't want to flame out. And I don't want this thoughtful young man to become embittered and disillusioned, either.

When we're perpetually angry, it's not just unpleasant for us and the people around us; it also takes a real toll on our physical and emotional health. An extensive body of scientific research has shown that sustained negative emotions harm the body, and ongoing stress can damage biological systems. Over time, this can lead to heart disease, stroke, and diabetes. Chronic anger can also lead to cardiac dysfunction by altering the heart's electrical stability.

"But negative emotions are only one-half of the equation," says Laura Kubzansky, Harvard School of Public Health associate professor of society, human development, and health. She explains, "It looks like there is a benefit of positive mental health that goes beyond the fact that you're not depressed. What that is is still a mystery. But when we understand the set of processes involved, we will have much more insight into how health works."

A 2007 study by Kubzansky and colleagues followed more than 6,000 men and women over two decades, and she found that emotional vitality—defined as having a sense of enthusiasm, hopefulness, engagement in life, and the ability to face life's stresses with emotional perspective and balance—appears to significantly reduce the risk of coronary heart disease. Her group's 2001 study also showed that more-optimistic people had about half the risk of getting cardiovascular disease as did those who were more pessimistic. Kubzansky and other researchers have been able to replicate these findings several times with different subjects.

At the core of her research is her strong belief that "everyone needs to find a way to be in the moment, to find a restorative state that allows them to put down their burdens." Our anger about racism is real. Our despair over sexism and White supremacism is legitimate. The planet is in crisis, too. Yes, yes, yes.

But we all need quiet moments to heal ourselves. Whether it's turtles on a trail, our dogs in our laps, or laughing uproariously with friends—we need these moments to sustain us emotionally and physically and give us the energy and grit we need to keep fighting the darkness.

The End of Nuance

§

FRANCE'S PLEYEL—the world's oldest piano maker—
recently announced that it would cease production
after 200 years of making superb instruments. Favored
by Chopin, Liszt, Ravel, and Stravinsky, Pleyels are known for
quality and innovation. Many French citizens lament the loss
of the workshop as an affront to French artistry and history.

According to an exhibition mounted in the Royal Academy
of Music Museum in London, Chopin once confided to a
student, "When I feel out of sorts, I play an Érard piano and
I easily find a ready-made sound. When I'm feeling ener-
getic and strong enough to find my own sound, I must have
a Pleyel." According to Joseph Bamat, journalist at the international news channel France 24, Chopin's appreciation for
Pleyel pianos was so strong that "he struck a sponsorship
deal similar to those between sports stars and apparel companies today; when in France he exclusively played Pleyel. . . .
In return, the composer always had free instruments at his

disposal." His Pleyel pianos were the tools with which he shaped pieces rich in subtlety.

A decade ago, Pleyel produced 1,700 pianos a year; last year its master artisans made only 20. Stiff competition from Asia, coupled with declining demand in the West, has shifted the market. More than half the pianos sold in the world last year were purchased in China. According to Tom Hundley of the *Chicago Tribune*, of the 480,000 pianos produced in 2008, a whopping 430,000 were made in Asia. Although most piano aficionados agree that Asian-produced pianos do not yet have the comparable sound and quality of venerable brands such as Steinway, Érard, and Pleyel, they are decent instruments at a quarter of the price. *Quel dommage!*

Pleyel has doggedly resisted abandoning nuance and subtlety for discounted, straightforward tones. When speaking with the *Tribune's* Hundley, Pleyel master builder Sylvan Charles explained what it takes to produce Pleyel's "round, warm, sensual sound": an additional thirty to forty hours of fine tuning in a "voicing room" with arcane tools and an exacting ear. "When it arrives in here, it is not yet a Pleyel. See, that's a Yamaha sound—very sharp and metallic. But when it leaves this room," he boasted, "it will be a Pleyel." This final tuning comes after 5,000 separate parts have been assembled by twenty expert artisans over 1,000-plus working hours. Is the resulting sound luscious? *Oui!* Is the public willing to pay for it? *Non!*

The French have unabashed and deserved pride in their history of fine piano making. For 200 years, French piano makers have tinkered with the best ideas from Britain, Austria, and Germany to produce incomparable instruments.

Pleyel artisans assert that their pianos' superior tone is due, in part, to the red spruce used for the soundboard. Not just any red spruce—north-facing trees of a particular age, thickness, and grain from the Fiemme Valley of South Tyrol in Italy.

Although quality has been a constant for Pleyel, so has financial trouble. "There has not been a large-scale factory for years, but the sadness comes from the death of a symbol," says Jean-Jacques Trinques, author of *Le piano Pleyel*, in a recent interview with Bamat. He notes that Pleyel took a real hit in the stock market crash of 1929, and although the brand survived, it passed through several hands—even moving production to Germany for more than twenty years. Pleyel did not return to Saint-Denis until 2000.

This is not really a story about the loss of French business, but more about the fear of lost identity. Anne Midavaine of the French Confederation of Art Professions, explained to *The Telegraph*, "Don't we sum up everyone's dream of France's grandeur, its non-exportable knowhow?" Pleyel represents a deep cultural appreciation for craftsmanship, deliberative art, and the hope that substance will triumph over cut-rate substitutions.

As Pleyel's Saint-Denis factory ceases production, another very different manufacturer on the other side of the world is going gangbusters. The *New York Times* reported last November that Venezuelan Eliezer Álvarez, in an effort to boost sagging sales, redesigned his female mannequins to—in his opinion—more accurately reflect the Venezuelan beauty aesthetic. They now have enormous, gravity-defying breasts and waists so narrow that they abandon the laws of physics and biology. Nuance and subtlety have been jettisoned entirely; these plastic forms are a celebration of artifice and the artificial—a brazen declaration that ersatz breasts trump unpresumptuous (natural) ones.

Slate editor Katy Waldman rightly argues that these "va-va-voom" dummies are really no worse than the unnaturally scrawny ones preferred in Europe and North America. But they do signal an in-your-face rejection of the loveliness found in the understated.

As Pleyel pianos represent France's self-identity as a once-great cultural powerhouse that exports grandeur and craftsmanship, Venezuelan mannequins assert an increasingly widespread cultural belief that "perfection" can and should be purchased through plastic surgery. Lauren Gulbas, an anthropologist at Dartmouth College, maintains that breast augmentations are popular in Venezuela because of a strong cultural belief that they convey perfection and *buena presencia* ("good presence"). Who needs to actually cultivate charisma when you can just buy double-D saline implants to captivate a crowd? There is absolutely nothing subtle about gigantic fake breasts.

Sophie Heawood, writer for *The Guardian*, muses that our movement away from embracing nuance might be nested in a growing social media culture that encourages binary thinking: "It goads us into pretending not to have nuance; to taking a stand on one side or the other of things." This trend has a tendency to suppress important questions about self, identity, and worldview. She concludes, "It's the nuances that keep us sane."

And, I would add, it's the subtleties that truly captivate.

The Secret Life of Humans

§

FEBRUARY 26, 2013

TRUE CONFESSION: I'm a Bette Midler fan. Wait! Stay with me for a moment. I'm not referring to Midler's sappy "Wind Beneath My Wings" phase. (I couldn't get through her "Beaches" period without a shot of tequila, and even then it was difficult.) I mean the unpolished Midler of the New York City bathhouse days: Sophie Tucker jokes and outrageous costumes like giant hotdogs and mermaids performing choreographed routines in motorized wheelchairs. Irreverent. Unpredictable. Creative. Edgy. Simply put: great fun!

You can't tell from looking at me that I will always carry a torch for that bawdy 1970s torch singer. When I told my eighth-grade English teacher that I intended to do my year-end biography project on "The Divine Miss M," Mrs. Edwards' eyebrows shot to the ceiling. "Well," she muttered, "we'll just check with your mother about that."

To my mom's credit, she's always appreciated my eccentricities. After a brief discussion, she ascertained that I was absolutely serious, so we went to the bookstore. She found a biography of Midler that didn't seem to have too many questionable sections—but, honestly, how do you clean up the story of the gay men's bathhouse scene in disco New York?—and she seemed just as excited about the project as I was. Who doesn't love a singer dressed as a giant frankfurter? My mom, the Kung Fu Fighting Grandma, has her own idiosyncrasies. She's equally comfortable wielding a fighting fan or singing with her choir at Carnegie Hall.

In my twenties, I hit a rough patch and was feeling somewhat lost. My brother invited me to go mining for Herkimer diamonds—double-terminated quartz crystals—in central New York. We packed up his tools, including an immoderately sized sledgehammer, and off we went. On a tiny plot of land that served as his refuge, he showed me the brute force—and tender finesse—required to coax one from the rock.

The beautiful metaphor of it all only now hits me; my brother has spent his entire life tending to diamonds in the rough. That day was a revelation. The light refracted ever so slightly and revealed a facet of my brother that had gone undetected for far too long: his ability to uncover beauty. I hold the memory of that day in reserve for those times when I need a touchstone for the essence of my brother. The sunlight, the clink of the tools on the rock, the syrupy scent of wildflowers and goldenrod at the edge of the property—all instantly bring to mind a time when I unearthed a deeper truth about this kind and complex man.

Sometimes the secret life of humans reveals itself in daily

rituals; you simply need to watch for it. There's a group of women at my gym. I call them "The Amazons." They gather together at dawn to put their bodies through a ghastly drill of weights, contortions, and grunting—all suffused with uproarious laughter. Thinking myself fit, I joined them for several weeks last year. But I simply could not keep up. Their "woodchopper" move—in which you swing a perversely heavy weight between your legs—just about did me in. Squatting, I found out, is an absolutely necessary move in one's life. So now I watch them, and gain inspiration, as I clock the miles on the treadmill behind them. These gutsy gals gather folks to them; their energy is potent. Although I don't know their day jobs, I imagine them as "Insurance Adjusters by Day, Amazons at Dawn." How many of their co-workers know of their secret fitness cabal? How many colleagues know that they dance with iron before the sun has properly shown herself?

I recently learned that a dear neighbor of ours who died this winter was a secret poet. I heard one of his poems at his memorial service; it tickled me that this diehard Yankees fan tucked a touch of the romantic beneath that well-worn baseball cap. Another neighbor lives for his hunting camp in the Kingdom but harbors a deep and abiding passion for the Beatles. It is the unexpected that sheds light on those deep and often hidden alcoves in which our whole selves dwell. This is the marrow of life.

When I taught undergraduate history, I assigned a book by Philip Deloria (son of famed Indian activist Vine Deloria Jr. and history professor at the University of Michigan) called *Indians in Unexpected Places*. Deloria's book invites us to expand our sense of what makes an Indian an Indian. He deconstructs archival photos of such seemingly incongruous images as Geronimo sitting in a Cadillac or a traditionally dressed Native woman perched under a hairdryer at the beauty salon. Deloria challenges our notions about Indians and their relationship to modernity. He asserts that Native people, like all Americans, have their own "secret histories." Far from being anomalies, Indians who engage with modernity and fashion it to their own purposes are simply claiming their right to be complex, fascinating Americans who flirt with the unexpected.

When we are honest with ourselves, we all want permission to explore, to yearn, to seek, and to find beauty in the unexpected. And when we share these hidden aspects of ourselves, we offer up an authenticity that is both captivating and comprehensive. Don't hate me because of my Midler fetish; see it for what it is: an affirmation that our incongruities are actually the very core of our humanity.

The Tonic of Wildness

§

I T STARTED with a friend's five-year-old son mischievously brandishing a bottle of water to sprinkle on another little boy's back. The "prey" dashed off, squealing and grinning, and the chase was on. Soon my own little rascal joined the frisky fracas, and the three boys scurried around the school's lawn like frenzied squirrels. I glanced at the parents in the group; we'd all spontaneously gathered at dismissal time, sharing pleasantries and animal crackers. No one tried to control the somewhat wild play. An unspoken understanding seemed to ripple through the group: They need this.

Soon more kids had organized themselves into spur-of-the-moment races down the subtle slope of the hill to the school's sidewalk. Again and again they raced. The dashes revealed an undeniable instinct to move. The kids made up their own rules and ultimatums; they argued over fairness and who was "boss." They ran, rolled, or just flopped down on the grass to steamroll each other. Their zip was enthralling, and—admittedly—sometimes barely controlled. After much gleeful gamboling, the three-and-under set wandered off to explore the school's garden, and some of the older kids scrambled up into welcoming tree branches. I checked my watch: nearly an hour had passed since dismissal. It was if we'd been under an enchantment. Romping in the outdoors can be like that—captivating and restorative. We don't do enough of it.

A study from the Institute of Social Research at the University of Michigan concluded, after carefully tracking the habits of over 2,000 families, that today's American kids, on average, spend only four to seven minutes a day in unstructured play outdoors outside of the school day. And school recess time itself has been drastically cut nationwide as schools have felt the crunch to adhere to the strictures of No Child Left Behind. Our kids' lives are much more structured and scheduled than the lives of children a generation ago; few have the opportunity to just "play" in the outdoors.

But outdoor play seems to be just what the doctor should order. A 2011 study published in *Applied Psychology: Health and Well-Being* tracked over 400 students diagnosed with attention deficit disorder (ADD) and monitored whether daily exposure to "green spaces" would help ameliorate symptoms. What the researchers at the University of Illinois Urbana-Champaign discovered was that regular exposure to natural settings significantly reduced symptoms of ADD in students. Drawing on the work of Rachel and Stephen Kaplan and their attention restoration theory (ART), the Illinois researchers discovered that, just as adults concentrate better after exposure to nature, so too do children benefit from regular exposure to natural settings.

The Kaplans were greatly influenced by the ideas of philosopher and psychologist William James, often referred to as the "Father of American Psychology." James asserted that humans have two different types of attention: voluntary and involuntary. We use voluntary attention, or directed focus, when we attend to a task that requires deliberate attention, like problem solving or driving in heavy traffic. But prolonged voluntary attention fatigues our minds. Conversely, James contended that certain elements of the natural world draw our involuntary attention—"strange things, moving things, wild animals, pretty things . . ."—and these do not require the same mental effort. Using James' framework, the Kaplans hypothesized that exposure to natural-world diversions greatly rested and restored our directed attention.

And simply moving our bodies—even indoors—also helps us to focus. A study presented in May at the conference of the American College of Sports Medicine found that fourth and fifth graders who exercised vigorously for at least ten minutes before a math test scored higher than those who sat quietly before the exam.

An acquaintance whose daughter attends the Chinese Immersion charter school in Hadley, Massachusetts, recently told me that her daughter gets regular exercise and "movement breaks" throughout the day. Although my mind immediately went to those unsettling Maoist mass-exercise drills that were shown on US news clips from China throughout the Cultural Revolution, it certainly makes sense to me that moving the body clears the mind. I could not focus enough to write this column each week without first feeding my exercise habit. And I would not survive the 3:00 to 5:00 P.M. "witching hour" of parenting without getting my kids outside; we are all "bears" then. Bears are decidedly happier moving their bodies outside than leaping from my couch and nearly missing the coffee table.

With the dramatic rise in the use of antidepressants among preschoolers—use among preschool age boys is up 64 percent in recent years—it is hard not to think that many kids simply need to be outside moving their bodies more. Richard Ryan, professor of psychiatry, psychology, and education at the University of Rochester, co-authored a paper describing four experiments indicating that the benefits of being outdoors are not simply salubrious. They also shape our values. Participants exposed to the natural world tended to be happier and demonstrated more generosity. They also rated community and personal connections as more important than those who did not spend time outdoors.

Although I would love to see all our kids in schools that resemble the Ewok village of *The Return of the Jedi*—glorious tree houses set amidst a lush emerald timberland—schools can't take this on alone. There are simply too many demands placed on schools already. Communities must come together to take the initiative. Some local examples include a group of families writing a grant to get playground equipment, a committee of parents and teachers who built a school greenhouse, and volunteers who helped create an outdoor classroom.

This Wednesday is International Walk to School Day. If you have neighbors who can't walk their young kids to school, offer to walk with them or help organize a group from your area to walk together. If you're a spry retiree looking for a workout, this could be the incentive you've been looking for. Get outdoors and move your body while modeling great habits for students.

As Henry David Thoreau insisted, "We can never have enough of nature."

Part Five

§

Justice

What Could Be More Important than a Man's Liberty?

❧

FEBRUARY 2, 2018

W E ARE A NATION of people who love courtroom dramas—*L.A. Law, The Practice, Matlock, Boston Legal,* and *Law & Order.* Jack Nicholson's quote from the 1992 movie *A Few Good Men*—"You can't handle the truth!"—is so well known that there are GIFs and memes of it that bounce around social media. We're riveted by stories that slowly reveal truth through bits of evidence, and we're thrilled by tales of high-stakes exoneration or condemnation. Just don't ask us to serve on juries ourselves.

When I recently served on a jury, I received a lot of sympathetic texts from friends about my predicament. Many asked why I didn't use my legislative position to "get out of it." And others said that my work in the Senate was more important; I should leave jury service to others who were not as busy. My spouse, an attorney, made an important observation to me as I fretted over whether I'd made the right decision to miss my work in the Senate for several days. She asked, "What could be more important than a man's liberty?" This framing distilled my jumbled emotions down to this basic truth: There is *nothing* more important.

During voir dire—the process through which jury members are chosen from the pool and asked questions about their beliefs and experiences—it became obvious which of my fellow citizens I wouldn't want sitting in judgment of me if I were ever charged with a crime. There were those who divulged that they were uncomfortable with the concept of "innocent until proven guilty": "He's been charged, so he's probably done something wrong." Others said that they'd think poorly of the accused if he didn't testify in his own defense. The judge stressed that our American system of jurisprudence is clear: not only did the defendant not have to testify, but we as jurors couldn't factor his decision not to testify into our deliberations about his guilt or innocence. Even then, several potential jurors didn't budge: "I'd still want to hear from him."

The process eventually winnowed us to fourteen jurors (including two alternates). We represented a true cross section of Windham County. We came from different backgrounds and experiences, but we were bound together into a semblance of community by virtue of our stated willingness to be open-minded about the case.

For several days, we were essentially asked to peek inside the lives of our fellow Vermonters—strangers in crisis—and reassemble a kind of truth. Yes, we were charged with gathering an accurate understanding and interpretation of events, but within that task was folded something larger. Pulitzer

Prize–winning poet Gwendolyn Brooks said it best: "We are each other's harvest; we are each other's business; we are each other's magnitude and bond."

In the days since my jury service, I've come to understand this in a much more poignant way. It's true that this experience bolstered my belief that we humans can still rise to a quiet greatness—even in uncomfortable moments when we're asked to sit in judgment. But the more potent realization for me has been that, nested inside each of our somewhat tidy public personas, there always stirs a messier conglomeration of experiences, emotional tides, and complex social networks.

I'm grateful that the act of sitting in judgment—of weighing evidence and searching for the heart of this one small case in the southeast corner of Vermont—has given me access to a robust compassion that is neither sentimental nor simplistic. My understanding of my community grew in proportion to my willingness to understand the importance of protecting a man's liberty.

Rough Sleepers in Paris

§

December 17, 2013

WHEN MY LAWYER SPOUSE was tapped to clerk for a federal judge in Casper, Wyoming, she couldn't turn down the prestigious post. An avid hiker, I was eager to spend a year closer to Yellowstone and Grand Teton National Parks but was less keen to relocate from my hip New England town with its excellent coffee and international restaurants. Although friends argue that my tastes veer to those of a seventh-grader—pizza, bagels, mac and cheese—I do have an abundant appreciation for fine java and crusty bread. I was delighted when I spied a French bakery in downtown Casper. Maybe I could make this Western experience work after all.

My elation was short-lived. A local told me that the shop would likely soon close. Embarrassed, she explained, "People have stopped going there. You know—part of the whole anti-French 'freedom fries' thing. It's terrible." She referred to the directive by the chairman of the congressional Committee on House Administration to rename french fries in the congressional cafeterias after France declined to support the proposed US invasion of Iraq to look for—as it turned out—nonexistent weapons of mass destruction (WMDs). Long entrenched, albeit relatively dormant, American anti-French sentiment was on proud display once again. Asked for comment about the freedom fries dustup, French embassy spokeswoman Nathalie Loisau remarked wryly that french fries were originally from Belgium. (You could almost hear the well-justified sneer: *"Imbéciles!"*)

American Francophobia has many roots. Americans sense that the French are not eternally grateful for the Allied liberation during World War II. The controversial British historian David Starkey asserts that French anger towards the Americans and the English stems from conflicted feelings over having been liberated: "People don't like being freed. They mistake liberators for conquerors." French historian Justin Va sse contends that the distrust has more to do with the missing Franco-American lobby in the United States; few Americans are of direct or recent French descent. Whatever the reasons, there is a nagging American belief that the French are just different. Sure, their incomprehensible love of Jerry Lewis's inane comedies sets them apart. But they are undeservedly mocked as somehow less manly, less virile—tending towards "blue-blood" instead of Red-Blooded American.

There is, however, one real thing that makes the French different: they have a deep compassion and affinity towards the homeless. Polls consistently show that French people are more sympathetic towards the homeless than residents of any other European nation. An astonishing 75 percent of French people surveyed in a 2009 poll said they felt "solidarity" with "rough sleepers" (the French colloquialism for the homeless), and 56 percent said that they feared they could be homeless themselves someday.

As Angelique Chrisafis, reflected in *The Guardian*, "The French are the nationality most likely to view homelessness as the result of financial crisis, unemployment, and housing crises and the least likely to blame the individual for personal reasons such as drugs or alcohol." Compare this to a 2011 American survey from the University of North Carolina at Chapel Hill in which 91 percent of respondents asserted that homelessness was primarily caused by drug and alcohol abuse; 62 percent said it was laziness.

There is also a gendered component to this issue. Like French nationals as a whole, a large percentage of American women fear that they could someday be homeless. The 2013 poll by Allianz Life Insurance Company of North America found that a full 27 percent of very successful women (those making over $200,000 a year) reported worrying that they might become destitute. A survey reported in Bloomberg supports these findings: women experienced more acute anxiety about finances than the men surveyed.

This complements the findings of a recent survey by the Public Religion Research Institute: American libertarians are overwhelming young, White, and male. Nora Caplan-Bricker, writing in the *New Republic,* argues, "The thing about freedom is that its heights are limitless, and its lows are bottomless. Libertarians, I presume, look at that void and never consider that they will do anything but rise." If you believe that boundless freedom surely enables success, you are less likely to support a social safety net. But if you assume that fortune can be fleeting and fickle, you are "all in" on a social contract.

Thus, it was refreshing to learn that a young, affluent, White male Parisian—Joël Catherin—took a stand for the rough sleepers in his neighborhood several winters ago. Using the ubiquitous, tattered cardboard signs that panhandlers the world over use to cajole loose change from luckier passersby, he forced Parisians to expand their already sympathetic hearts even more. He noticed a homeless elderly woman in his neighborhood suffering through a bitterly cold winter night. Instead of her usual sign, "I am hungry," he made her a new sign that read: "I could be your grandmother." It worked wonders; many more people gave money. I do wonder why he didn't invite her in for a warm croissant and hot *café au lait*— but hey, we do what we can when we can.

He began to make clever, eye-catching signs for homeless people all over Paris and started a citywide discussion. "It wasn't about money," he explained. "It was about changing the way people view others." At a basic level, of course, compassion can be stirred within us when we feel a kinship with someone in distress, when we stop viewing an individual or a group of people as somehow different from ourselves. In this way, I hope to become a bit more French.

Journalists Protect
the Rule of Law

§

JULY 18, 2018

"THIS IS WHAT HAPPENS when a reporter refuses to give up on a story." The *Columbia Journalism Review* posted this on Twitter last week in reference to the excellent work of *Miami Herald* investigative journalist Julie K. Brown and her reporting on the sex-trafficking crimes of financier Jeffrey Epstein. Brown's four-part series in the *Herald* was instrumental in bringing to light a very disturbing plea deal that Epstein's high-powered lawyers cut with federal prosecutors back in 2008. Epstein's now back in custody; the former federal prosecutor, Alexander Acosta, just resigned as Trump's secretary of labor; and finally—after an indefensible and agonizing wait—Epstein's hundreds of victims will be heard. None of this would have happened if Julie Brown and her colleague, visual journalist Emily Michot, hadn't doggedly researched the case.

Although other journalists decided that the Epstein story was stale, Brown dug back in after President Trump nominated Acosta to join his cabinet in 2017. As the US attorney in Miami, Acosta had overseen Epstein's prosecution. Brown told the *New York Times* recently, "Sometimes a story deserves a new look." Indeed.

Brown started with a highly redacted 100-page police report that contained references to over 100 Jane Does. She poured over the report for bits of information that would help her identify these girls. She then created a spreadsheet of alleged victims and got to work tracking them down for interviews. Brown said of her process, "There were all of these puzzle pieces that were out there, and when you put all of these puzzle pieces together, with the passage of time, there was this really damning story."

This—*this*—is why we must have a free and open press. Journalists like Brown are the people's watchdogs, not the enemy of the people as Donald Trump claims, echoing totalitarians of the past. Brown often asserts that she's not the hero—that the real heroes are the brave women who spoke out about the abuse they suffered at the hands of Epstein and his many accomplices when they were in their teens. Of course, she's right. But Brown used tenacity and skill to unify and amplify their voices so they could no longer be ignored. If Brown and photographer Michot hadn't pursued this story and published their four-part series "Perversion of Justice" back in November, Epstein would not be back in custody, and his victims would not have had the opportunity to speak out in court at Epstein's bail hearing in New York on Monday.

As in 2008, Epstein's lawyers again argued that Epstein should be allowed to await trial in his own gilded cage. They offered that Epstein could post $100 million for bail. He should then be confined to his luxurious Upper West Side townhouse, they said; Epstein would pay for round-the-clock monitoring by a private security firm. Assistant US Attorney Alex Rossmiller pushed back: "What the defendant is asking for here is special treatment, to build his own jail."

And why wouldn't he ask? It worked last time. After he pleaded guilty to prostitution in 2008, Epstein served his sentence in a private wing of the Palm Beach County stockade instead of in a Florida state prison. But he basically only slept there; he was allowed work-release privileges and sometimes didn't return to the lockup until ten o'clock at night. His money and powerful connections enabled him to make his own rules; normally, those who are registered sex offenders are not eligible for work-release privileges.

Journalists like Brown are the last line of defense against this kind of abuse of power. She recently said that, in addition to fighting for justice for Epstein's victims, she hoped her work "has helped the public see we're not the enemy of the people."

Will We Reject the Moral Rot?

§

NOVEMBER 26, 2018

I UNDERSTAND WHY so many Americans, although concerned—even scared and outraged—by journalist Jamal Khashoggi's murder, feel so overwhelmed by the sheer number of public transgressions by this president. But I urge all of us to not become inured to the horror and not to be distracted by other embarrassing (but less substantive) statements or missteps by this president.

As usual, there have been numerous times in the past week when I've felt embarrassed by President Trump: the rambling press conference in California in which he misnamed the town that had been destroyed in a horrible, surreal conflagration; his public, childish attack on the Navy Seal who led the operation to capture Osama bin Laden; and his personal attack on a federal judge because of the judge's ruling on asylum-seeking immigrants. There were so many other awkward moments, inappropriate tweets, and bald-faced lies that grabbed national attention. As painful as it is to witness, there is some small comfort in knowing I'm not alone in my mortification.

According to a Quinnipiac University Poll from earlier this year, a majority of Americans are embarrassed by our commander-in-chief. And 67 percent of Americans believe that Trump has a negative impact on the nation's children. So it's clear that many of us feel a deep shame about this president. But Trump's public statement about the Khashoggi murder must shift our dismay and distress firmly into the column of rank disgust. While he acknowledged that the crime was a "terrible one," he went on to say that the priority was to maintain a good relationship with Saudi Arabia. It is deeply shocking. Please, let it shock you.

Feel the weight of the wrong. Please, shake your head in disbelief. Do not let Trump normalize a premeditated murder and dismemberment of a human being inside a consulate by a US ally. Our president didn't just side with autocrats. He didn't just give cover to Saudi crown prince Mohammed bin Salman (MBS). His public statement made clear that he values a (vastly exaggerated) trade deal with the Saudis more than a human life. He is comfortable with his own moral rot. But more than that, he wants us to be comfortable with it, too.

Fred Ryan, publisher and chief executive of the *Washington Post*, boils it down to stark, chilling terms: "Flash enough money in front of the president of the United States, and you can literally get away with murder."

Ryan also perfectly dissects a critical aspect of the president's official statement on Khashoggi's grisly murder; Trump argues that some in Saudi Arabia viewed Khashoggi as an "enemy of the state" and a member of the Muslim Brotherhood. The president then says, ". . . but my decision is in no way based on that." Ryan astutely points out that Trump employs "a rhetorical device known as paralipsis—saying something by professing not to say it." When Trump does this, he unabashedly asserts that the Saudis were justified in luring the journalist into the Saudi consulate in Istanbul in order to kill him and chop up his body. Ryan goes to the heart of it for me when he writes that this "makes me want to throw up."

A man—a journalist, a father, a fiancé—was lured into the consulate under the impression that he was securing documents so he could marry. He never came out.

Some in my social media newsfeed have argued that we should not be shocked. They cynically say our personal and collective dismay over Khashoggi's killing (and our president's refusal to confront the truth) reveals a naiveté about the world. They hide behind a kind of sloppy moral relativism that uses our own nation's previous atrocities as a justification for heinous Saudi actions. I reject this, and I urge you to reject it as well. Our words create our world.

Post-Gender? Not a Chance.

❦

October 12, 2017

A FRIEND RELAYED a conversation she'd had with a male politician recently. He said he didn't really support the efforts of Emerge Vermont, a left-leaning political training program for women candidates; he believes there's no need for it. "We're post-gender," he remarked—or some such nonsense. He wasn't saying we have moved beyond gender identity or commenting on the empowerment of transgender people. No, it simply wasn't a priority for him to elect more women because, he explained, women have already made so many strides. He also didn't think that electing more women would change political conversations.

One need only look at the train wreck that is the Affordable Care Act (ACA) repeal movement to see that it is an *extremely* gendered issue. When the first Obamacare repeal bill was drafted by Republicans in the House of Representatives, not a single woman was involved in the drafting. The result? Women's health care needs were essentially ignored. The bill was a direct assault on cancer screenings for women, basic gynecological care, reproductive health, and pregnancy-related health care.

As I've discussed before in this column, poverty is also a gendered issue. Across the country, women are much more likely than men to live in poverty. Women are still paid less than men—even decades after this issue first became a battle cry for feminist activists. In terms of housing, one of the biggest demographic groups in desperate need of affordable housing is single moms with young children. Women are drastically underrepresented in Congress (we make up 50.8 percent of the American population but only 27 percent of Congress) and in corporate board rooms across the country. Just about any political issue one examines has a gendered aspect to it. It's simply ludicrous to say that we're "post-gender."

Even our late-night talk shows are extremely gendered in their humor. I'm a big fan of Trevor Noah, Seth Meyers, Jimmy Kimmel, and Stephen Colbert. I think our comedians are actually doing some of the most courageous, insightful political commentary in these deeply disturbing times. I start my day by reading several newspapers; then I stream the late-night comedians' new commentary while I make dinner. With the entry of Samantha Bee into this arena, I've become much more aware of just how often the others' commentaries are focused around the male experience. And male genitals. Noah, Meyers, Kimmel, and Colbert almost always have at least one phallus joke in their routines—and often more than one in each show.

This became even more noticeable to me when Seth Meyers added a segment on his show called "Jokes Seth Can't

Tell," starring Meyers and two of his female staff writers: Jenny Hagel and Amber Ruffin. Ruffin is Black and Hagel is gay and of Puerto Rican descent. They tell the punchlines of jokes that Meyers feels uncomfortable telling as a straight White man. The juxtaposition of these jokes with the usual late-night fare helps illuminate the extent to which the usual jokes are grounded in and shaped by a male perspective.

I deeply appreciate these comedians and their daring, spot-on candor about our political mess. But I think it's important that we acknowledge that the jokes are primarily written by men and geared toward a male audience. Only 18 percent of writers on the eleven most successful late-night talk shows are women. This clearly has an impact on their jokes.

We're not post-gender, folks. We haven't reached parity; we're not even close. I know that when any group starts to gain more political power—even a modest amount—those who've had that power for so long feel threatened. And when they give voice to those feelings, they say things like, "We're post-gender." It is not true yet—but let's work to make it so.

Sterling and Silver

§

FOR THOSE OF YOU who still held out hope that the nation that elected President Obama is a "post-racial" society, the news out of Los Angeles last week was an abhorrent reminder of the tenacity of racial prejudice. Donald Sterling, owner of the NBA Los Angeles Clippers franchise, made headlines when his surreptitiously recorded boorish racial rant went public. On tape, he tells his former girlfriend that he doesn't want her to post pictures of herself on social media in which she poses with black people. He clearly should spend more time worrying about his own image.

A friend recently commented that Sterling looks like the love child of Jack Klugman and Jabba the Hutt; still, like Jabba, the billionaire real estate developer clearly had clout. Now that the spotlight is more finely attuned to Sterling's disgraceful record of past prejudice and "plantation" mentality, former Clipper general manager Elgin Baylor—who unsuccessfully sued Sterling for racial discrimination—will finally feel vindicated. And NBA commissioner Adam Silver's maximum fine and lifetime ban of Sterling sets a new tone of complete intolerance for racism within the NBA. But why did it take so long?

Sterling, whose lackluster team has long been the butt of jokes, was well known throughout the NBA—and beyond—for racism. But recently, after his team finally started to win games, the NBA and the public seemed to have tacitly accepted that, although he's a bigoted lout, at least he now runs a winning franchise. All's fair in victory and profit? Gene Demby, of NPR's *Code Switch* podcast, points out that Sterling's $2.7-million settlement of a lawsuit brought by the Justice Department because of discrimination in his rental properties was the largest payout ever for housing discrimination. After the settlement became public, the NBA issued no fines or sanctions against Sterling and seems to have wholly ignored the issue.

Although the tape recording was a smoking gun, there has been enough smoke hovering around Sterling for years that someone higher up in the NBA should have long ago yelled, "Fire!" Jay Jaffe, writing for *Sports Illustrated,* points out that Major League Baseball took on Marge Schott—former Cincinnati Reds owner—when she made repeated offensive comments about Blacks, Jews, and women. Schott was the first woman to purchase a controlling share of a Major League Baseball team, but her "status as a pioneer," writes Jaffe, "was buried amid her limitless capacity to offend." Like Schott was to baseball, Jaffe argues, Sterling is a blight on the NBA. Commissioner Silver must be unwavering and methodical in rebuking owners and coaches for repugnant statements and actions.

My backdrop to this Sterling and Silver scandal has been David Levering Lewis's celebrated biography of Black historian, sociologist, and intellectual W. E. B. DuBois. I purchased Levering Lewis' two-part biography of Du Bois (each of which won the Pulitzer Prize for biography) years ago, but had not finally cracked them open until last week—just days before Sterling's disturbing comments. After finishing Annette Gordon-Reed's recent biography of Andrew Johnson, I felt compelled to dive in.

As Reconstruction foundered under President Andrew Johnson, and the nation began its horrid slide into Jim Crow and unconscionable violence, there were, as always, incredible stories of Black men and women who wrought better lives for themselves—lives lived among people who would have them disappear or be shipped to Africa's distant shores.

Reading the inspiring story of W. E. B. DuBois, I marvel at his talent, curiosity, and drive. DuBois never doubted that he had what it takes to achieve academic greatness—despite constant reminders from a nation unwilling to truly grapple with hundreds of years of exploitation and underestimation of Black people. DuBois, like all his Black contemporaries, yearned for respect in the broken, but not chastened, South and the gritty, unforgiving North.

Certain moments in the text force rumination on the depth and scope of suffering shaped by the weighty fear of difference. When DuBois and his wife lose their two-year-old son to diphtheria, they follow behind the cart carrying the tiny coffin to the Atlanta train station to be brought home to Great Barrington, Massachusetts. Even while engulfed by profound grief, they are not afforded any propriety or solemnity. White onlookers shout, "Niggers!" as they walk in a haze of sorrow and loathing. The year is 1899; the Civil War has been over for decades and yet freedom never coalesces; it is a noble notion, unrealized. Because emancipation is not simply about manumission; it is about freeing the spirit and allowing it to live up to its true potential.

DuBois labored his entire adult life to reframe society's beliefs about Black people and their capacity for intellectual achievement. Much has been made of DuBois's clash with contemporary Booker T. Washington over whether Black people would find salvation through hard work and industrial education or by rigorous classical study. But this famous disagreement should not obscure DuBois's most important principle: the conviction that all men should have "intelligence, broad sympathy, knowledge of the world that was and is, and of the relation of men to it" in order to fashion a "true life." Every man must balance the "skill of hand and quickness of brain, with never a fear lest the child and man mistake the means of living for the object of life."

Despite Donald Sterling's delusions of grandeur as a modern NBA plantation master lording over his Black "slaves," he is but a "boy." I mean "boy" spoken with the full weight and scorn of lifetimes of derision that DuBois and millions of others have endured at the hands of ignorant men who never fully embodied the wisdom and understanding of the brotherhood of man.

That's "Mr. President" to You

§

I N 2009, Aretha Franklin created a minor scandal with her headgear at President Obama's inauguration. Her stunningly large hat bow—so big it nearly blocked the view of luminaries sitting in the grandstand—was all anyone could talk about for weeks afterwards. Although many criticized the bonnet as being too much for the occasion, Franklin demonstrated her respect for President Obama by essentially dressing in her Sunday best. Surely a hat that she would wear to church to worship the Almighty appropriately demonstrates respect for a new president.

At President Obama's second inauguration, another bold, talented Black woman is in the hot seat. This time, Beyoncé has been criticized for singing along to a pre-recorded rendition of our national anthem. Although her decision to lip sync may seem at first to smack of laziness or impertinence, her choice actually indicates her deep respect for the president—something distressingly missing inside and outside the Beltway.

When the Queen of R-E-S-P-E-C-T first heard about Beyoncé's lip-synching, she reportedly threw her head back and laughed. Franklin said she almost wished she'd made a similar decision four years earlier. Franklin wanted to perform perfectly for the president, as did Yo-Yo Ma and Itzhak Perlman. They, too, played along to prerecorded music for President Obama's first inauguration, but it didn't become a national scandal. As Yo-Yo Ma told *New York Times* reporter Daniel Wakin at the time, "What we were there for was to really serve the moment." Perlman felt similarly: "The occasion's got to be perfect. You can't have any slip- ups."

Last week, Beyoncé echoed these sentiments: "Due to the weather, due to the delay, due to no proper sound check, I did not feel comfortable taking a risk. It was about the president and the inauguration." But she wasn't afforded the same latitude as were the titans of classical music. This could be because she once performed in the unfortunately named pop group Destiny's Child, but I think that's racism. Many feel that she, like the president himself, simply doesn't belong at the inauguration at all.

As I watched the Beyoncé dustup unfold, I recalled an interview that NPR's Ari Shapiro had with a Romney supporter during the last presidential election. She'd complained vociferously about President Obama: "I just—I don't like him. Can't stand to look at him. I don't like his wife. She's far from the First Lady. It's about time we get a First Lady in there who acts like a First Lady and looks like a First Lady." In a subsequent interview, she insisted that her comments had nothing to do with race, but there's something about "Can't stand to look at him" that highlights the real subtext. Like others in the American electorate, she believes that Black people have gotten above their station.

Remember the reprehensible T-shirt that popped up at an Ohio campaign event for Romney? "PUT THE WHITE BACK IN THE WHITE HOUSE." Remember Sarah Palin's racially charged critique of Obama that he was "shucking and jiving" about the terrorist attack in Libya? Or the absurd, insistent chatter about President Obama's birth certificate; or South Carolina's US House representative Joe Wilson calling the president a liar during a joint session of Congress; or Mike Huckabee and Newt Gingrich's race-tinged accusation that Obama has a "Kenyan mentality"? (On this last point, even conservative *Washington Post* columnist George F. Will voiced his concerns that such comments are so bizarre that they hurt the Republican Party.) These examples merely legitimize the flood of racist tweets on Twitter following Obama's re-election and on the occasion of his Sandy Hook memorial speech.

Last year I spied an anti-Obama bumper sticker on a car in downtown Brattleboro that whipped my head around. It read, "B.O. stinks." The "O" incorporated the same font and design that was used in Obama's campaign literature. In almost the identical spot, years earlier, I'd spotted another bumper sticker: "Somewhere in Texas, a village is missing an idiot." Although equally disrespectful to President George W. Bush, the latter at least lacks a racial subtext about cleanliness and hygiene.

Retired Colonel Lawrence Wilkerson, and onetime chief of staff for former secretary of state Colin Powell, said in an

MSNBC interview last fall, "Let me just be candid. My party is full of racists." Responding to former New Hampshire governor John Sununu's claim that Powell only endorsed Obama because he's Black, Wilkerson argued that Sununu's beliefs are not singular. "The real reason a considerable portion of my party wants President Obama out of the White House," he asserted, "has nothing to do with the content of his character . . . and everything to do with the color of his skin." Wilkerson, clearly disgusted by this pernicious tendency in his own party, has no clear idea what, exactly, to do about it, but I respect him enormously for naming the problem. There are legitimate reasons why true fiscal conservatives would oppose Obama's presidency; there must always be room for lively, substantive dissent. But, as Wilkerson asserts, the GOP's "big tent" must not become a refuge for bigots.

All American presidents are demeaned and mocked by pundits, the press, and other politicians. It's tricky to balance respect for the president of the United States with our nation's abhorrence of monarchical pomp and circumstance. George Washington was initially addressed by the affected and unwieldy title: "His High Mightiness, the President of the United States and Protector of their Liberties," which he roundly rejected as antithetical to the principles of the Revolution. James Madison—the little big man dubbed the "Father of the Bill of Rights"—put an end to that. Although the first vice president, John Adams, complained that "Mr. President" was not deferential enough, the title stuck.

Sometimes I wish that "his High Mightiness" were still in use. I'd love to see Arizona governor Jan Brewer's facial contortions as she struggles to get the words out. Governor

Brewer, who demonstrated contempt and impudence when she wagged her finger in President Obama's face last year, would not be the only one to choke on the glorious title. But hey—if it really became a struggle for her, she could always lip-sync it.

The Past is Present

§

Mississippi's US Senate race garnered little national attention until Republican Cindy Hyde-Smith—appointed to complete the term of Thad Cochran—made several eyebrow-raising statements in the waning days of the special election called when Cochran resigned his office due to failing health. Hyde-Smith quipped about her willingness to attend a public hanging (in an odd show of affection for a campaign supporter) and said she'd support making it more difficult for "liberals" to vote. She dismissed these comments as "jokes" and won the election by 8 percentage points. "Wink and nod" politics and policies that support White supremacy have held sway in Mississippi since Reconstruction.

In the final days of the election, we learned that Hyde-Smith attended a segregation academy and also sent her daughter to one. Segregation academies opened throughout the South after the 1954 US Supreme Court ruling *Brown v. Board of Education.* White Southerners circumvented the desegregation of public schools by founding thousands of private schools—often funded in part with public dollars. Hyde-Smith attended the now-closed Lawrence County Academy in Brookhaven, Mississippi; she sent her daughter to Brookhaven Academy, which is filled almost entirely with White students, although Brookhaven's population is 55 percent Black.

Brookhaven is no anomaly. According to a 2012 Southern Education Foundation study, only 50.6 percent of school-age students in Mississippi are White, but White students make up 87 percent of private school enrollment.

Indeed, little has changed since 1972, when a young lawyer from Yale named Hillary Rodham was sent to Alabama by Marian Wright Edelman—the famed civil rights activist who founded the Children's Defense Fund. She went undercover as a young mom looking for reassurance that the school she was considering for her son would not be integrated. Later, in her book *Living History*, Hillary Rodham Clinton recalled: "I was assured that no Black students would be enrolled."

In *Brown v. Board of Education,* the US Supreme Court ordered states to end segregation with "all deliberate speed." But fifteen years later, the Court had to order thirty school districts in Mississippi to integrate immediately. Mike Espy, Cindy Hyde-Smith's Democratic opponent in the Senate race there, was one of the first Black students to integrate the Yazoo City High School after that 1969 ruling.

Today, the Yazoo City Municipal School District is 98 percent black. Like many public schools in Mississippi, it is underfunded and ranks low on nearly every performance measure in the state. Espy finished his high school years just before the massive "White flight" to the segregation academies.

When he was sent to Congress to represent Mississippi's 2nd district, Mike Espy became the first African American elected to Congress by Mississippi voters since Hiram Revels served from 1870 to 1871. Revels was one of over 1,500 Black officeholders during Reconstruction, but their political power was fleeting.

Almost immediately after Reconstruction ended with the withdrawal of the last Federal troops in 1877, there began a period disgustingly dubbed "Redemption" by White Southerners who called for the return of White supremacy even as they dismantled Reconstruction reforms, terrorized Black people throughout the Deep South, and stripped them of newly gained civil rights. If you're over forty, you probably received a very slanted view of this important time in our nation's history. The version of Reconstruction that held sway for years across this nation was told exclusively from the point of view of the Southern planter class.

Accurately understanding the Reconstruction period helps us more fully grasp the politics still in play today. Read one of Eric Foner's great books on Reconstruction or W. E. B. Du Bois's masterpiece "Black Reconstruction in America." At the very least, watch the short video series put out by Facing History/Facing Ourselves. (You can find it at www.facinghistory.org.)

The past is ever present. And until we accept that, we can't chart a more just path forward for this nation.

The Right to Fear

§

I WAS NOT AT ALL SURPRISED by the verdict in the heart-rending Trayvon Martin case. It was, devastatingly, exactly what I'd expected.

Rich Lowry, editor of the conservative *National Review*, asserted in an op-ed last week that the Trayvon Martin case was never about race. Lowry called the trial of George Zimmerman—the Sanford, Florida, neighborhood watch volunteer who shot Martin—"the racial metaphor that failed" and "a tale of the left's desperation to indict contemporary America as a land of rank racism." Although I agree with him that comparing the death of Trayvon Martin to the lynching of Emmett Till—for supposedly whistling at a White woman in 1950s Mississippi—is not an entirely apt comparison, it was astonishing that Lowry would dismiss the presence of race and its critical importance to the context and complexity of this particular case. What set the tragic events in motion was Zimmerman's belief that Martin—a Black teen visiting family in the neighborhood—had no legitimate reason to be in his gated community; Martin's youth, his clothes, his class, and the color of his skin were all signals to Zimmerman that Martin was someone to fear.

The trial hinged on the jury's interpretation of the struggle that precipitated Martin's death. Who was on top? Who was the aggressor? Whose voice is heard screaming for help on the 911 tape? Race, central to the national discussion since Martin's death, was relegated to the sidelines in the courtroom. As *New York Times* reporter Lizette Alvarez asserts, "The judge made it clear that statements about race would be sharply limited and the term 'racial profiling' not allowed." This is partly due to Florida's overly generous self-defense laws, which protected Zimmerman even though he precipitated the conflict by tailing the innocent Martin before confronting him. But racial issues should not be ignored. Zimmerman's four other calls to the police to describe suspicious people in his neighborhood all reported Black people. His fear and distrust were certainly shaped within the context of race and class.

New York Times columnist Charles Blow wonders whether we are "acculturated to grant some citizens the right to feel fear while systematically denying that right to others." Zimmerman's attorney pounced on prosecution witness Rachel Jeantel when she recounted that Martin told her he was scared because he was being followed by a "creepy-ass cracker." The defense lawyer suggested that it was Martin who was racial-profiling, not Zimmerman. It seems that an unarmed, young, Black male—being followed at night by a stranger—is not entitled to feel genuine (and, it turns out, justified) fear for his life. Even if Martin was the one who initiated the physical altercation, it is certainly true that the two need never have been in close contact. Blow reminds us that "if Zimmerman had stayed in his vehicle and not pursued the teenager, Martin would have made it home for the second half of the NBA All-Star Game."

A 2007 Justice Department study reveals that although Black people make up just 13 percent of the American population, they are the victims of almost half of all murders in the United States; three out of four of these murders are committed with guns. Dan Eggan of the *Washington Post* asserts that "encounters with criminals are often more likely to turn deadly for Black victims than for victims of other races, in part because Black victims are more likely confronted with firearms." Blacks in poor or urban areas were more likely to be victimized than those in affluent areas. Yet Zimmerman was culturally entitled to his fear but Martin was not.

I taught English in El Salvador for a summer in the late nineties. On a day trip to an outlying village, I went walking on a trail on the outskirts of town with two friends, an American and a Salvadoran. We each tucked a few colones in our pockets in case we needed to hand over some cash quickly to any thugs. We were prepared for muggings, but our Salvadoran friend assured us that we'd be safe with her—especially in broad daylight.

As we strolled along chatting, a young man suddenly emerged from behind a tree, brandished a pistol, and said, "*Disculpa.*" (I'd been mugged before in Manhattan, and I can assure you no one ever said, "Excuse me.") It was an odd moment; it took us several beats to realize he was accompanied by two men with machetes. They waved the machetes threateningly and, although my fear prevented me from quickly translating the Spanish they shouted at us, there was no mistaking their meaning. They grabbed our goods and slipped back into the woods while we ran for our lives.

Afterwards, as we tried to calm our nerves and drive out all the awful images of what could have happened, my American friend and I assessed our losses: some money, our watches, and our feelings of invincibility. But our Salvadoran friend had, by far, lost the most. Her work briefcase was gone; it contained just about every cherished monetary possession she had, along with keys to her office and home. She was devastated—truly scared for her safety. Deconstructing the events, we all agreed that our race and our social class had certainly put our Salvadoran friend at much greater risk than if she'd been walking with other Salvadoran friends.

By failing to fully consider the complexities of race, class, and gender, or the fact that our mere presence as Americans signaled wealth, we had unwittingly made her a target. We should have thought about these things; we were living in a foreign country. Not so for Trayvon Martin. He assumed he'd be safe in a familiar neighborhood in his own country.

Part Six

❦

Action

Akin, Putin, and a Russian Punk Band

§

AUGUST 28, 2012

L AST WEEK, just several hours after I submitted my column—on the rather ho-hum nature of the 2012 presidential race—Missouri congressman and U.S. Senate candidate Todd Akin's dizzyingly ignorant remarks about rape, pregnancy, and abortion changed the political landscape. When asked whether he believes that abortion is justified in cases of rape, Akin responded: "It [pregnancy following rape] seems to be, first of all, from what I understand from doctors, it's really rare. If it's a legitimate rape, the female body has ways to try to shut the whole thing down." Not surprisingly, Americans reacted strongly and swiftly on social media platforms to his mention of "legitimate rape."

Now the establishment wing of the GOP wants him out; he's repeatedly vowed to stay in; and incumbent Democrat Claire McCaskill just might eke out a victory in a state that a few weeks ago favored Akin by 5 percent. Democratic candidates across the nation are seizing on his comments in order to bolster their campaigns, while Republicans are publicly denouncing him in an effort to save their own skins. Akin's remarks certainly deserve all the attention, but it's revealing that it took such absurd comments about women's reproductive health to draw attention to the uncomfortably cozy relationship between Evangelicals and right-wing discourse in this country.

In an interesting convergence, the same week that Representative Akin unwittingly started a mass uprising over female anatomy, members of the female Russian punk band Pussy Riot were criminally sentenced for their public rant/ prayer protesting Vladimir Putin's re-election. The protest occurred on February 21, 2012, when five women from Pussy Riot entered the Cathedral of Christ the Savior of the Russian Orthodox Church in Moscow. There was no church service in session. They removed their winter clothing, donned balaclavas, and walked up the steps leading to the altar. The women jumped around, and punched the air for less than a minute, and were then escorted out of the building by guards. Film footage of this performance was then used for a video clip for one of their songs, "Punk Prayer: Mother of God, Drive Putin Away." The women were sentenced to two years in a penal colony.

Putin's use of the Russian Orthodox Church to prop up his oppressive oligarchy in Russia is not so very different from Congressman Akin's attempt to use his own narrow religious views to greatly restrict women's reproductive rights in the United States. One would think that Akin, who—like vice presidential candidate Paul Ryan—believes that all abortions should be banned, would also adhere to the

"Let's-get-those-commies" shtick that has been a mainstay of American conservatism for decades. But there's been a palpable shift lately as the more extreme wing of the Republican Party seems to feel some kinship with the autocrats.

According to a 2011 Gallup Poll, only 20 percent of Americans believe that all abortions should be illegal. Even a big chunk of those who identify as "pro-life" believe there are some circumstances in which it should be allowed. Yet Akin believes he represents a silent majority of Americans who would condone a police state to enforce an outright ban on all abortions. His views, taken to their logical conclusion, would lead to a society in which neighbors rat on neighbors; patients turn in health care providers; extremists target "rumored" abortion providers; and women die from botched, unsanitary procedures. Regardless of your personal views on abortion—and let's admit that the issue is both complex and highly emotional—most Americans do not wish to live in a country resembling a KGB-enforced police state that sends patients and doctors to prison or fines them for making highly personal health care decisions.

We tend to feel superior when we ponder the Russian electorate's willingness to bring an autocrat like Putin back to power. Nick Cohen of London's *Observer* argues that "Putin offers the Orthodox Church a partial restoration of its tsarist privileges," and that Orthodox patriarch Kirill I "returns the favor by making support of the Kremlin . . . a quasi-religious duty." But just as Putin looks to Kirill for continued support to legitimize his power, so too in America do ultra-conservative Republican candidates seek power and legitimacy from Evangelical Christian leaders with their particular interpretations of Christian thought. In fact, there is no universal agreement among American churches and synagogues on the issue of abortion, but some political candidates talk like autocrats: theirs is the one legitimate view and they will impose it on everyone—regardless of federal law.

The American right quickly condemned Pussy Riot's punk prayer in Moscow's Cathedral of Christ the Savior, calling it an example of blasphemy and nihilism. (Given that they're part of a "twenty-something" punk art collective, isn't it kind of their job to be nihilistic?) There has been no similar condemnation of Putin's autocratic rule or a denunciation of the Orthodox patriarch who calls the Russian president a "miracle of God." (Talk about blasphemy!) Tom Bethell, senior editor at the conservative *American Spectator*, seemed rather envious of the Kremlin when he wrote in a piece entitled "Blasphemous Chic" that "the Russian leadership and the Russian Orthodox Church are moving closer together and won't be entertaining the 'separation of church and state' anytime soon." Further, Bethell's defense of the Orthodox patriarch is revealing in light of Kirill's statement that the "human rights concept is used to cover up lies, falsehoods, and insults against religion and national values." Cohen highlights that in Kirill's book, *Freedom and Responsibility: A Search for Harmony*, the patriarch vociferously denounces secular countries that allow women to control their own fertility; those who disagree with him are tools of the "puppet masters" who follow "Jewish philosophers." Kirill's anti-Semitic blame is eerily reminiscent of a sign I once saw at an abortion protest rally in the early 1990s: "Jewish doctors are butchering Christian babies."

Some new-wave American Republicans seem comfortable with more autocratic control over the lives of American citizens—as long as they're the ones tailoring and enforcing the restrictions. Akin represents a highly energized movement of (mostly) male, paternalistic politicians who believe they must protect women from themselves. They inject religion relentlessly into political debate without seeing the irony, and we continue to let them do it.

Several years ago a Russian friend of ours, who now teaches at an American university, remarked that Americans were entirely too smug about our freedoms. She argued that she saw plenty of Americans with latent fascist tendencies. I thought it was hyperbole at the time. Now I'm not so smug.

A Contagion Threatening Democracy

§

JULY 11, 2019

PRESIDENT TRUMP'S Independence Day gaffe—
claiming that during the American Revolution the
Continental Army seized control of the airports—
provided great comic fodder for late-night talk show hosts,
meme-makers, and my own history-loving children. It was
an outrageous blunder, but most public figures know when to
smile, sheepishly admit the mistake, correct it, and then move
on. Not so this president. He is incapable of copping to any
errors, regardless of their magnitude. This scares the hell out
of me.

I've written on the horrors and the stark meanness of many
of Trump's policies, and I've discussed his fascist tendencies,
as well as his admiration for despots and his embrace of kleptocracy. I'm deeply weary of this terribly flawed president and
his rampant incompetence. I've expressed my alarm that he
surrounds himself with people who enable the abuse of power

and continue to prop up a man who has built his career on fetid tommyrot. But this president's inability to admit to and correct a mistake or misstatement terrifies me the most.

What does it say about a man when he cannot admit to any mistakes? And what does it say about our nation that millions of people still support this president after thousands (literally, thousands) of lies, half-truths, and complete fabrications? There's a contagion threatening our democracy. It didn't start with Trump, but his presidency has shown us—in vivid technicolor—that we have collectively created a body politic that craves a particular kind of leadership, rooted in absolutes and wrapped in bluster. We have little appetite for intellectual humility anymore.

Michael P. Lynch, a philosophy professor at the University of Connecticut, has written about the dearth of intellectual humility. He's also the principal investigator of the group Humility & Conviction in Public Life, which (according to its website) is a research project "aimed at revitalizing our fractured public discourse." Lynch exhorts us to balance our strong convictions with a healthy curiosity about what we might be getting wrong. But he concedes that this is challenging to do when we live in a culture infatuated with arrogance.

Lynch has written several books and many essays, including "Teaching Humility in an Age of Arrogance," which appeared in the *Chronicle of Higher Education* in June 2017. He writes, "Trump is a symptom and not the cause of a larger trend, one that rewards dogmatic certainty and punishes those who acknowledge the possible limitations of their own point of view." He asserts that Trumpism flourishes because of a potent cultural cocktail: technology, psychology, and ideology. And because of the complex and pervasive interaction of these factors, it's exceedingly difficult for individuals to push back.

The algorithms used by most internet search engines and social media platforms steer particular information towards us that often reinforces our beliefs. And if we're already prone to believing that we know more than we actually do, this is a dangerous pattern that bolsters our ignorance. And then, of course, there is the frightening rejection of any objective truth. As Lynch aptly points out, "Skepticism about truth is really more self-rationalization than good philosophy. It protects our biases" and makes it easier for us to overlook our own ignorance. And, ultimately, it makes the ground fertile for despots.

I have little hope for Trump or his toadies. But the rest of us must challenge ourselves to embrace more intellectual humility. Start from a place of rational conviction. Then accept that your view can be improved and refined by the contribution of others. Listening deeply and thinking critically are antidotes to the pre-existing conditions—bigotry, fearfulness, and unreflective arrogance—that enable Trumpism. It is these individual actions by thousands of Americans that will help cure the contagion.

Deconstructing "Madame No"

§

JULY 10, 2012

THEY CALL HER "the Iron Frau" or sometimes simply "Madame No," but according to last week's news, German chancellor Angela Merkel seemed to be uttering a "maybe." For months, Merkel has rejected calls for Eurozone debt sharing and Germany's continued role as the Eurozone's ATM. At the most recent European Union summit, however, Merkel gave tepid support to debt sharing among EU partners—with strings attached. Merkel, the de facto leader of the European Union, leads the most powerful economy in Europe at a time when the ambitious Eurozone experiment is precariously close to collapse. World markets impatiently await her next move; many wonder why she has been unyielding on this issue, and why she might be wavering now.

Because of her center-right politics and her advanced degree in science, Merkel is often compared to another influential former prime minister, Great Britain's Margaret

Thatcher. But her most striking similarity to Thatcher is her steely resolve. Thatcher famously said, amid enormous pressure to ease the economic reforms her party put in place in the United Kingdom in 1980, "To those waiting with bated breath for that favorite media catchphrase, the 'U-turn,' I have one thing to say: 'You turn if you want to. The lady's not for turning.'"

Similarly, despite extreme pressure from governmental leaders across Europe, Merkel has long rejected collective European debt sharing over fears that it would leave Germany holding the bag. As Jeremy Warner, associate editor for *The Telegraph* in London, has reflected, "Angela Merkel isn't bluffing. Like everyone else in Europe, she's defending national sovereignty." Merkel's refusal to pool debt in the European Union is not surprising, given the long line of European nations asking for bailouts lately: Ireland, Greece, Italy, Spain, Portugal and now Cypress.

She insists that Germany will not support collectivizing debt through issuance of euro bonds until strict economic reforms are enacted in Europe's debtor nations. She has been accused of being obstinate—and of protecting Germany's interests at the expense of the European Union. But there is another way to view Merkel's position and ideology: she is a product of her family's experiences and her nation's troubled history.

Although born in Hamburg, in what was then West Germany, Merkel moved to Templin, in East Germany, when her father, a Lutheran minister, was posted to a pastorate at the church in Quitzow. Gerd Langguth, a former senior member of Merkel's Christian Democratic Union party, asserts in his Merkel biography that her father had a "sympathetic" relationship with the Communist regime; this is the only legitimate explanation for why the family owned two automobiles and was able to travel freely between the two Germanys—significant privileges in the austere East. As the family shuttled between East and West, Angela Merkel lived the stark differences between communism and the free market. This surely shaped her worldview and cultivated in her a desire to see economic and political reforms in the East.

Merkel's Lutheranism also helps to explain her stance in the current economic crisis. Her refusal to overlook the profligate spending, and in some cases the fraud and dishonesty, of governments in southern Europe harkens back to Martin Luther's zealous reform of the Catholic Church five hundred years ago. While Luther confronted what he perceived as the corruption and unconscionable spending of the Roman Catholic Church, Merkel rejects the rampant spending and book-cooking of the governments of the Catholic states of Italy, Spain, and Portugal. According to Gavin Esler of the BBC, she represents the German taxpayers, who really want to be good Europeans at heart—just as Martin Luther wanted to be a good Catholic. "But in their heads, most Germans suspect that there may be something wrong—something morally wrong as well as economically dangerous—about giving money to those who . . . have been at best reckless and at worst dishonest."

Lutheranism alone does not explain Merkel's resistance to aligning Germany's future with that of the bankrupt Mediterranean economies. Remember those bizarre photographs in your high school history textbook of Germans wheeling wheelbarrows of all-but-worthless cash around to purchase sundries after World War I? Germans alive today remember what that economic misery led to: unbridled scapegoating and the rise of the Third Reich.

Because we are such a young nation, often perceived on the world's stage as a posturing teen, not an elder statesman, we often forget that history matters deeply in shaping individual and collective psyches. Throughout the Eurozone crisis, Germans as a whole, and Angela Merkel in particular, have been accused of smugness by their less successful European partners. But Germany is Europe's export powerhouse, so perhaps they are entitled to be smug. Moreover, who can blame them for being afraid of their own primal instincts? As Germans and all Europeans recall vividly, Germany's economic turmoil between the two world wars led to history's most extensive and effective killing machine. That's difficult to forget.

Immediately after the most recent European Union summit, Merkel was portrayed as having finally given in to the demands of Spain, Italy, and France for economic relief through more EU debt sharing. But with more time to reflect, analysts are coming to understand that Merkel essentially walked away with exactly what she wanted: in exchange for much-needed cash, France agreed to transfer supervision of its banks to the European Central Bank, which is located, unsurprisingly, in Frankfurt, Germany. Markets will continue to watch Europe closely. In the end, the Germans—with Merkel at the helm—will lead by pragmatic and savvy concessions. They will have to concede some things, but it will be on their terms.

Garden-Variety Demagogue

✄

MARCH 21, 2019

IN THIS WEEK OF PURIM, I'm reminded of how tempting it often is to have easily identifiable villains and scapegoats. That was certainly the main thrust of President Trump's painful speech in front of CPAC—the Conservative Political Action Conference—several weeks ago, immediately following the Hanoi Summit with Kim Jong-un. The rambling, off-script monologue included revisiting the size of the crowd at his inauguration in 2017, describing the need to remove leaf debris from the forest floor to stop wildfires, and claiming that the Democratic governor of California, Gavin Newsom, said Trump was a great president and one of the smartest people he'd ever met. Elisabeth Kübler-Ross's ubiquitous "Five Stages of Grief" describe how I struggled to come to terms with the president's performance.

Denial came first: The president couldn't really have delivered a two-hour-long speech of blathering nonsense. Then came anger: Who—in addition to Trump himself—can we blame for this horrifying display? Next was bargaining: If I give to the right candidate and knock on enough doors in the next election, I can assuage my despair. Depression soon followed: Trump's presidency is an indication of our deep moral rot; we're all doomed. Then I settled into acceptance: We have a demagogue-in-chief, and many Americans seem to love what he's peddling.

This admission is a milestone, although a deeply painful one. And we'll be better able to confront the beast if we start from there.

Trump has been called a lot of things since he first entered politics (e.g., bigot, narcissist, clown, idiot, bully, liar), but despite how apt many of them are, the sheer volume of the descriptors has had the unintended impact of muddying the issue. The constant blatant lies, race-baiting, sexism, fear-mongering, profound incompetence, arrogant bluster, and willful ignorance are all so horribly offensive. And it's true that we've not seen the likes of this before in a modern US president. But his playbook is not new. Trump is a garden-variety demagogue.

Like so many leaders before him, Trump appeals to the passions and prejudices of the masses instead of using rational argument. His oily charisma and creepy claptrap connect to the darker recesses of our feelings—and, unfortunately, we all have these weaknesses: resentment, suspicion, aggression, anger, and gobs of fear. His incendiary messages are neither clever nor novel; he just happens to have more potent media tools at his disposal than the demagogues of old could employ.

Trump's blame-filled "word salads"—maddening and embarrassing to many of us—are also appealing to a significant swath of the electorate. Dr. Saul Levine, psychology professor emeritus at the University of California, San Diego, explains why: people "respond to a demagogue as if he were a savior who will destroy their enemies, bring back 'the old values,' and most of all, help them feel better about themselves and their world." Simply put, we crave a sense of belonging, and a demagogue's easy answers and targeted blame offer relief to those feeling powerless.

This is obviously a potent political force to counteract because it's so resolutely not based in facts or verifiable knowledge. And, unfortunately, it's a byproduct of democracy itself. So, what can any of us do to combat demagoguery?

It starts with each of us. Regardless of political stripe or ideology, we must be watchful and not accept easy answers for difficult problems. When we give in to simple, dangerous narratives about groups of people and their political ideas, we're no better than Trump when he demonizes the press, immigrants, Muslims—or his chosen enemy of the week.

We must constantly, publicly reject dangerous demagoguery in our elected officials and leaders while simultaneously being wary of our own unsavory tendencies towards self-righteousness and angry condemnation for relatively minor transgressions. This acknowledgment of our own shortcomings offers a space for true connection with our neighbors and friends who hold different opinions. It's imperative that we continue to push ourselves to make and cultivate connections with those with whom we disagree. These relationships will become critically important reminders to reject fear and anger when another populist leader comes along and tries to dehumanize our neighbors.

Let's leave the simple, uncomplicated stories of good and evil to times like Purim, when we recreate the vanquishing of a brutal dictator and the only weapons we need to employ are noisemakers and costumes.

Families Belong Together

§

*This column is an excerpt of a speech the author
gave on June 30, 2018, as part of a rally for the
Families Belong Together campaign.*

TODAY'S EXTREME HEAT reminds me of when I
lived in San Salvador, El Salvador, twenty years ago.
The long, brutal civil war had recently ended, and I
lived in a city and a country still traumatized by death squads
and grinding poverty. Yet, despite seemingly insurmountable
obstacles, my friends there retained their hope and their spirit
and their belief that they could and would make a better life
for themselves and their children.

In the evenings, through intense heat and often under a
light rain, we'd walk down to the local *pupusería* to share food,
stories, and sometimes song—those shared experiences that
bind us together. Those meals provided actual sustenance as
well as a beautiful spiritual sustenance. For a few hours, we
left the violence and despair on the streets outside to remind
each other of the joy that comes from sharing in each other's
humanity.

But as we all well know, violence begets violence, trauma produces trauma. Although the civil war was over, the horrors didn't simply disappear. The damage didn't instantly evaporate when a peace agreement was signed and a new political era began.

The trauma remains.

The museums and memorials dedicated to the victims showed the trauma in stark, unfiltered details. I saw binders of photographs taken at the grisly scenes of murders perpetrated by government forces against civilians. Visitors were forced to directly confront the violence, the trauma, and the lack of humanity. We could not look away. We had to live with our nausea, our grief, our profound despair. We had to integrate what we'd seen and find a way to use these feelings, this knowledge, to continue to fight for justice and to not shut down.

Look around you at this crowd. You are here today because you won't look away. You see the horror at our own border. You're here because you allowed yourself to look, to see, to admit that our own government is perpetrating this great wrong against families and children who come here for refuge. And you know that the trauma will not go away when these children are reunited with their families. That is the hardest part for me—knowing that even after we shut down this horrible practice, the trauma will persist.

The great political philosopher Hannah Arendt wrote about totalitarianism and how to push back against the forces of evil. She wrote: "Action is never possible in isolation; to be isolated is to be deprived of the capacity to act."

This is my guidepost today. I will not lose my capacity to act. Despair and heartache must not close us off from each other.

But something is happening, something is shifting. The horror is stripping away our self-consciousness. Our collective heartache is producing a new, profound sense of connection. On the streets of this town, people—many of them strangers to me—are stopping me to tell me of their sadness, their horror, their feelings of despair. They seek community.

We must hold each other's despair. We must listen and acknowledge the feelings of sorrow and fear. And then, my friends, we must continue our work. Those families at the border need us. The children suffering through trauma and poverty in our own communities need us. And yes, those who are perpetuating violence and trauma need us to free them from the horrible part they're playing in all this suffering.

In short—we need us. Thank you for being visible when invisibility is easier. Please take care of yourselves and each other. The arc of justice is long, but this is the journey we are called upon to take.

I'm so grateful that we are on this journey together.

Conspiracy Theories:
Fighting Fire with Water

§

NOVEMBER 29, 2019

C ONSPIRACY THEORIES have been around for as long as there have been people to concoct them, but there's been a notable shift in what they look like and how they operate. Recently I've felt wholly ill-equipped to battle the disinformation that's being disseminated throughout our body politic these days.

Some recent conspiracy theories have been painfully absurd: Hillary Clinton running a child-sex-trafficking ring in Washington, DC, at a pizza shop ("Pizzagate"). Horribly offensive: The mass shooting of children in Newtown, Connecticut, was staged by actors in order to strengthen the case for gun control. Absolutely politically motivated: Climate-change denier, Senator James Inhofe (R-OK) said, "With all of the hysteria, all of the fear, all of the phony science, could it be that man-made global warming is the greatest hoax ever perpetrated on the American people?" Inhofe spreads a conspiracy theory by claiming it's all a conspiracy theory. This is tough stuff to combat.

Professors Jan-Willem van Prooijen of Vrije University in Amsterdam and Karen M. Douglas of the University of Kent in England have developed a construct to help us understand why and how conspiracy theories come to be accepted. Their research suggests that the aversive and acute emotions that people experience when in crisis—fear, uncertainty, and loss of control—prompt a strong impulse to attempt to make some sense of the situation. This appears to increase the likelihood of perceiving conspiracies as real.

We can debate what the current crises are in our nation that contribute to the spread of conspiracy theories. Economic fears? Perceived loss of power by those who've held it for so long? Shifting mores around sexual orientation, gender identity, and gender roles? Acute wealth disparity? The beginning of a long-overdue national reckoning with racial injustice? Certainly these all play a part.

But regardless of the particular factors in play, there are similarities in the psychological function these theories have for those who believe in them. As van Pooijen and Douglas highlight, they give people easy answers and offer up somebody to blame. This provides a sense of control—albeit a false one—for people experiencing the world as uncontrollable.

So conspiracy theories aren't new, and they address feelings that most of us have. What is different is that conspiracy theories today can start as false statements tweeted in an instant by fabulists like our president and weaponized through multiple social media platforms. Many are also not grounded in any facts whatsoever.

Nancy L. Rosenblum of Harvard University and Russell Muirhead of Dartmouth College authored *A Lot of People Are Saying: The New Conspiracism and the Assault on Democracy* (Princeton, 2019). They assert that the newest conspiracy theories are different and dangerous because they are "conspiracy without the theory." As Rosenblum and Muirhead explained in a recent interview in *The Economist*, "Its proponents dispense with evidence and explanation. Their charges take the form of bare assertion."

The authors concede that it's tempting to fight this fire with more fire—spewing our own counterfactual humbuggery. But that doesn't address the real danger to our democracy that conspiracy theories pose, and it "obliterates a common world of facts and public reasoning." Instead, we must douse the flames with a constant, unrelenting demand for facts and supporting evidence.

This is something we all can and must do. We should demand this of our politicians, local leaders, activists, and journalists—and also our friends and family. When we see folks veering into the realm of conspiracy—whether on the Right or Left—we must gather our courage and confront this problem head on. Assess why the theory might be appealing to that person and identify the emotions it soothes or inflames. Then be unyielding in your determination to insist on evidence. It is not hyperbole to say that our republic depends on us to do this work.

The Great Migration

§

JANUARY 26, 2018

I TRAVEL A LOT to and from Montpelier, and although the early-morning or late-night trips can sometimes be exhausting, I often cherish the solitude. My little hellions at home are two very creative and spirited Huns who leave me little room for quiet reflection. But when I'm in my car and can stream a podcast, in minutes I'm lifted into a heady realm of calm and potent intellectualism. My framing of the world is stretched, and I'm grateful for the expansion of my understanding. This week it was Krista Tippett's excellent National Public Radio show *On Being* that carried me into the sublime.

Tippett interviewed Isabel Wilkerson, the Pulitzer Prize–winning author of *The Warmth of Other Suns: The Epic Story of America's Great Migration.* Wilkerson, the former Chicago bureau chief of the *New York Times,* took fifteen years to write this book, interviewing over a thousand people in the process. Upon its release in 2010, it became an overnight sensation, and in 2012, the *New York Times Magazine* included it in its list of All-Time Best Books of Nonfiction. The following year, the *New York Times Book Review* declared that "it shows every indication of becoming a classic."

The book chronicles the lives of three Black people who were part of the Great Migration, the mass movement of over six million Black people out of the rural South to the urban Northeast, Midwest, and West that occurred between 1916 and 1970. In her extensive interview with Tippett, Wilkerson tells Tippett that the frequent reaction of readers to her book is: "I had no idea this happened." As a historian who focused my research on Native American history and Post-Reconstruction Black history, I'm not in this camp. But I'm excited that Wilkerson has beautifully connected the saga of the Great Migration to conditions on the ground now.

As Wilkerson tells Tippett, "Our country is like a really old house. I love old houses. . . . But old houses need a lot of work. And the work is never done. And just when you think you've finished one renovation, it's time to do something else. Something else has gone wrong. And that's what our country is like." She warns us that we may not want to go into the "basement" of our country's past, but an unwillingness to do so comes at our own peril. Whatever we ignore will get worse, and we'll have to reckon with it eventually. She invites us to face that reckoning bravely.

Tippett's conversation with Wilkerson is a rich mix of history, sociology, and personal narrative. Both these women are recipients of the National Humanities Medal, and their conversation is at once complex and accessible. Reflecting on the power of Wilkerson's book, Tippett asserts that "it embodies this paradox that writers know, that storytellers know . . . that the more particular you can get with your story, the more universally it can be received, and others can join their life and their imagination with what you have to share."

Wilkerson's beautiful narrative adds to our understanding of this period in history and the people who shaped it. But her meticulous reconstruction of this epoch, coupled with the experiences of her protagonists, also helps bring much-needed context to our comprehension of the conditions that Black people face today.

The Great Migration was a product of the economic and political caste system in the post-Reconstruction South, but this tremendous movement of people toward a refuge—for their personal safety and a chance to realize their political identity—did not complete the work to be done. We still have so much do. Their courage to seek freedom must be matched by our own.

Hadestown: What We Need Right Now

§

JUNE 14, 2019

I'LL BET I FEEL like a lot of Vermonters this week: extremely disappointed that I didn't get tickets to see *Hadestown* while I had the chance. Vermonter Anaïs Mitchell's show *Hadestown* ("The Myth. The Musical.") won eight Tony Awards on Sunday night, including Best Musical and Best Original Score. Now it will be nearly impossible to catch the show, but I'm still so delighted for Mitchell and for all of us. Her beautiful work and her adept political commentary give me hope in these extremely distressing times.

The show is a clever retelling of the Greek myth of Orpheus and Eurydice; Mitchell sets the story in a Great Depression–era jazz club and the Underworld reimagined as a subterranean factory. It started as a DIY (Do It Yourself) community theater project; it morphed into a bluesy folk-opera concept album that Mitchell released in 2010; and it was then workshopped off Broadway in Edmonton and London before making its debut on the Great White Way.

One of the most memorable and haunting songs in *Hadestown*, "Why We Build the Wall," is a tune that Mitchell wrote around 2006 for the first draft of what would eventually become her hit Broadway show. It's sung by Mister Hades, the boss-king of a bleak Underworld factory, to his workers in a call-and-response style. Mitchell explained in a 2016 *Huffington Post* editorial piece that Hades uses the song to indoctrinate the people: "The Underworld is not the land of the dead, but . . . a walled city whose citizens engage in mindless, soulless work in exchange for the security promised by their boss-king, Mister Hades."

Hades: Why do we build the wall? / My children, my
    children / Why do we build the wall?
Workers: Why do we build the wall? / We build the wall
    to keep us free. / That's why we build the wall. / We
    build the wall to keep us free.

It's not surprising that, as *Hadestown* grew in popularity, fans began to ask Mitchell whether President Trump was the inspiration for "Why We Build the Wall." But, of course, when Trump was rising in the polls in the primary and the general election, the song was already over a decade old.

Mitchell explained, "I never expected it to feel new again. And then Donald Trump came along. It wasn't just that Trump made the building of 'the Wall' central to his initial platform, it was the call-and-response style chants at his rallies: Trump: 'Who's gonna pay for the wall?' Crowd: Mexico!'"

As I've written before in this column, Trump's demagoguery is vapid and old hat. He just deftly and relentlessly taps into timeworn fears and archetypal ideas of good and evil.

What's been very surprising for so many Americans is that we thought we'd moved beyond these banal, simplistic views of the world and its people. Tragically, though, we still seem stuck in these pathetic old paradigms. As Mitchell reminded us, "There is nothing new about the Wall. Political leaders have invoked it time and again to their advantage because it works so well on people who feel scared."

Mitchell wants us to understand that in *Hadestown*, unlike in the original myth, Eurydice is able to make a choice. And she chooses the security and safety that Hades offers her behind the Wall. Although Eurydice doesn't actually die, she has, of course, lost much of her life by agreeing to such a limited existence. It's as simple as this, explains Mitchell: "By walling others out, the citizens of Hadestown wall themselves in—to hell."

Mitchell's success with *Hadestown* is a huge personal accomplishment, but her triumph feels like a victory for thousands of us across this state who reject the isolationism espoused by our own Hades-in-Chief.

Language as Historical Thread

§

OCTOBER 28, 2014

I'VE BEEN CLOSELY FOLLOWING Chris Deschene's bid to become president of the Navajo Nation. Deschene was set to face former Navajo leader Joe Shirley in the general election, but several defeated primary candidates protested his inability to speak fluent Navajo. Navajo tribal law requires presidential candidates to be fluent in both Navajo and English, and although Deschene claimed in candidate paperwork that he was fluent, he now admits that his facility with Navajo is not flawless.

Deschene was then disqualified from the race after refusing to take a Navajo language proficiency test. He appealed to the Navajo Supreme Court, but his case was dismissed on a technicality. This week the Navajo Nation Council, the legislative branch of the Navajo government, will consider removing the language requirement for presidential candidates, so he still has a shot to stay on the ballot. Deschene's troubles have highlighted a growing divide within the Navajo Nation:

many younger tribal members do not feel that the language requirement is in the best interest of the Nation, while most elders feel it is critical to the Nation's cultural survival. The tension is made all the more compelling because the Navajo Nation and its language played a critical role in World War II with the celebrated Navajo code talkers.

Professor Manley Begay Jr. at Northern Arizona University, a member of the Navajo Nation, believes that a Navajo president must be able to speak the language because he or she must be able to communicate with older tribal members— some of whom speak only Navajo. But there's another reason why retaining a culture's language is so important: we learn important information about the past through clues that a language provides. For example, Robert Rogers' raid on the St. Francis Catholic mission (called Odanak in Abenaki)— home to hundreds of Abenaki Indians during the French and Indian War—demonstrates how important details are forgotten when historians and ethnographers ignore oral tradition and the nuance of language.

Rogers' own version of the October 4, 1759, attack on the village claims that he and his Rangers, aided by a group of Stockbridge Indians, raided a war-mongering group of Abenaki and killed hundreds of warriors. Later portrayed in the Spencer Tracy film *Northwest Passage,* based on the novel by Kenneth Roberts, that account stands in stark contrast to Abenaki oral traditions about that traumatic attack.

In his seminal 1972 work "Oral Tradition as Complement," the late anthropologist Gordon M. Day set out to resolve several key aspects of Robert Rogers' personal account of the raid that did not match French documents. For instance, Rogers insisted that hundreds of Abenaki were killed; French internal documents consistently recorded thirty dead (twenty of whom were women and children). Did Rogers exaggerate to please his superior officer, British commander Lord Jeffery Amherst? Or might there be another reason why his account differed so greatly from those of French eyewitnesses?

Day consulted a number of accounts from the Abenaki oral tradition to tease out important details about the raid. One came from the elderly Elvine Obomsawin, who shared it with Day in 1959. She heard it as a little girl from her aunt, Mali Msadoques, who in turn had heard it from her grandmother. The story of Malian Obomsawin, a little girl in the village at the time of the St. Francis Raid, had been passed down through generations of Abenaki women. The oral tradition tells of a teenaged girl who left an autumn harvest dance at the gathering hall to get some fresh air. While outside, she was approached by a stranger—an Indian, but not an Abenaki—who warned her that enemies had surrounded the village and would soon attack. The girl alerted the others, and most hid in a nearby ravine, thus saving a large number from certain death.

Day corroborated Obomsawin's version of the story by consulting another obtained from an elderly man named Theophile Panadis, who heard it from his grandmother, Sophie Morice, born in 1830, who in turn had heard it from villagers who were alive at the time of the raid. Not only does Panadis's oral tradition confirm that there had been a warning delivered to the residents at Odanak, but it also provides tantalizing clues as to the identity of the warner. On the surface, it makes no sense that a Stockbridge Indian would betray Rogers and warn the Abenakis. As Day explains, "The Stockbridges had suffered at the hands of the French and were fierce partisans of the English throughout the war." But if one considers the exact words uttered by the warner—as passed on through generations of Odanak Abenakis—it is clear that he was not Stockbridge; his language was close enough to Abenaki to be intelligible.

Day translates for us: "My friends, I am telling you." *Ndapsizak, kedodermokawleba.* (Abenaki: *Nidobak, kedodokawleba.*) "I would warn you." *Kwawimleba.* (Abenaki: *Kwawimkawleba.*) "They are going to exterminate you." *Kedatsowi wakwatahogaba.* (Same in Abenaki.) Both Day and University of Pennsylvania anthropology professor Marge Bruchac conclude that the Indian who gave the warning to people of Odanak was Samadagwis, the supposedly Stockbridge scout who was the only member of Rogers' party to be killed during the raid. Samadagwis was mostly likely a Schaghticoke—and not a Stockbridge—due to his language and the fact that he requested baptism before he died from his wounds. He was clearly not among the Stockbridges who were longtime followers of Puritan John Edwards.

I have reread Day's work dozens of times, and every time it gives me goose bumps. By honoring the power of oral tradition and attending to the specificity of language, he enables us to reach across time and hear accounts that solve longstanding historical mysteries.

It is up to the voting members of the Navajo Nation to decide if their president must be fluent in Navajo. But whatever the outcome of this race, it is critical that greater efforts be made within the Navajo Nation to preserve their language. We all lose some of the vital complexity of history when language is lost.

Lessons from a Pre-Columbian Phone

§

JUNE 17, 2014

I T LOOKS LIKE one of those string-and-paper-cup tele-
phones that children often make, except that it's over
1,200 years old. The receivers are made of gourds coated
with resin and stretched animal hide, and the seventy-five-
foot-long cord is fashioned from twined cotton. Writer and
historian Neil Baldwin calls it "a marvel of acoustic engi-
neering" that arose out of the Chimú Empire at its height.
He explains that the "dazzlingly innovative" Chimú culture,
centered in the Rio Moche Valley in northern Peru, was con-
quered and subjugated by the Incas around 1470, This was
sixty years before the Spanish conquistador Francisco Pizarro
attacked the Incas and several decades before the Columbian
Exchange radically hastened the flow of ideas between Europe
and America. It is the only example of this kind of phone ever
discovered in this part of the world from this time period.

Anthropologists guess that it was made only for elites in
the rigidly hierarchal Chimú society. Ramiro Matos, curator

at the National Museum of the American Indian and a specialist in cultures of the central Andes, speculates that the phone may have been made for executive-level communication between a lower-level assistant and someone of superior status. But, honestly, we'll probably never know why it was invented. The importance for me, as someone who earned one of my master's degrees in Native American history, is that it demonstrates ingenuity and inventiveness—qualities we often deny to indigenous peoples.

Culturally, politically, and emotionally, we are sometimes guilty of imagining Native peoples in a sort of suspended animation—unchanged by the exchange of ideas between societies and individual people. In many Hollywood depictions and storybook representations, Native Americans are portrayed as stuck in time—not allowed to adapt new technologies to their purposes or adopt and refashion others' ideas and traditions. Like any human beings the world over, Native American cultures are—and have always been—resourceful, imaginative, and practical. It is unfortunate and so very limiting to our idea of human ingenuity when we insist that Native groups remain "museum quality," as if they themselves were artifacts.

As part of my graduate school research, I studied the case of the Mashpee Wampanoag as they sought federal tribal recognition. They began this process in 1976 when they filed a claim in federal court for their traditional lands. Federal tribal recognition didn't come until 2007—over thirty years later. One of the biggest obstacles in their quest to regain their land was that opposing counsel argued that they couldn't truly be Native American anymore because they had adopted the ways of non-Native residents. Members of the Mashpee were put on the witness stand and interrogated about their dress, religion, and culture. Their integration of aspects of modernity was seen as evidence that they were no longer truly Native American.

This is not a uniquely American phenomenon. While I was in graduate school, a professor told me of a fascinating documentary another grad student had made about German attendees at Native American powwows. In the film, the tourists approached Native people to critique their style of dress and complain that it wasn't "authentic" enough. In one exchange, a German man insists that a Native American man's ceremonial clothing is not genuine because it is a mixture of old and new styles. He felt entitled to define true "Indianness" and to tell this man he fell short.

Once I traveled up to the Medicine Wheel in the Big Horn Mountains of Wyoming—an ancient site sacred to Native peoples throughout the Big Horn basin. On that day, a group of local Native American women gathered for a religious ceremony. Although it is classified as a National Historic Landmark and is managed by the National Park Service, the site is temporarily closed to tourists when Native Americans wish to use the sacred space. I waited about an hour before I was allowed to hike up to the holy site on the edge of a magnificent vista. Later, when I described my experience at the Medicine Wheel to a Caucasian acquaintance, she exclaimed, "Isn't it cool that we still have real Indians out here? Not like back East, where there are none."

It was a remarkable comment for so many reasons. First, glaringly, there was the "we" she used that perhaps suggested something akin to ownership of an entire people. There was also an implied tone of pride that Native Americans in the West are somehow more legitimate because many still live on reservations and have not intermarried with non-Native people to the extent that the Eastern indigenous people have done. I pointed out that Eastern groups still very much exist—despite 400 years spent in survival mode.

Following the Pequot War that ended in 1638—a war in which hundreds of Pequots were burned alive by the English and many of the survivors were sold into slavery by their English and Native American enemies—their tribal name itself was made illegal. For many Eastern groups, survival meant going underground. But even when survival is not immediately at stake, all people must be afforded the right to adapt and transform aspects of modernity.

Prize-winning writer and historian Philip Deloria—a member of the Standing Rock Sioux Tribe and son of Native American writer and activist Vine Deloria Jr.—has written several influential texts about the persistent attempts of non-Native people to dictate what is true and valid "Indian-ness." His 2004 monograph *Indians in Unexpected Places* challenges stereotypes of Native American people that restrict them to an unchanging past in which they are not allowed to adapt and repurpose modernity to their needs.

In one section of the book, "Expectation and Anomaly," Deloria deconstructs one of his favorite photographs from the 1940s. In it a Native woman in traditional buckskin beaded dress sits under a large salon hairdryer while she receives a manicure. Deloria asserts that the reason why so many people still chuckle at this image is because we believe subconsciously that "Indians live in the hinterlands, strangers to the urbanity of the manicure. They practice barter or gift economies and are, thus, unprepared for the cash exchange of the beauty parlor." When we laugh at such images as "anomalies," it's because it is easier to imagine them as exceptions rather than as an absolutely normal aspect of Native American culture—indeed, all culture. We all dabble, adapt, transmute, and borrow. And in the process, we automatically lose neither our identities nor our histories.

Someday we may discover more clues as to the inventor of the ancient cup phone. But for now, I am grateful for both the reminder about the elemental drive to innovate and the opportunity to imagine the cultural exchange and personal ingenuity that led to such a clever invention.

Rambling among the Ruins

§

AUGUST 25, 2017

A S I WRITE THIS, journalists across the globe are still trying valiantly to weave the president's rambling, incoherent, contradictory speech in Arizona into a somewhat cogent whole that will help us decipher the Trumpian roadmap. One thing remains clear: when Trump feels cornered, he fully embraces unmitigated nonsense. Case in point: this administration's (and do I ever use that term loosely!) desire to appropriate $3.6 billion over the next two fiscal years to construct a border wall with Mexico. There's a monstrous mound of evidence that the president is not beholden to the truth, even to his own past statements on the issue, much less to logic or—dare I even state the horribly obvious?—to researched facts and figures. And, clearly, his fans don't concern themselves with gross, glaring inconsistencies or the president's shameless opportunism. What Trump continues to do is play to naked fear, to the base instincts of his base.

The border wall is an incredibly powerful symbolic and physical bulwark against "the Other." It suggests safety and security for those seeking easy answers, those desperately clinging to the notion of a tidy world where nuance and complexity are simply tools of a shadowy, dastardly elite. A wall signals division; it indicates that differences, ways of life, are irreconcilable—that we are so at odds with each other that we must demarcate a tangible barrier to prevent being overrun and despoiled. And yet we know intuitively— if we are brave enough and honest enough to acknowledge the truth—that walls don't solve problems. They simply underline them.

It's been 100 years since Robert Frost published his poem "Mending Wall," but it feels as fresh and as relevant today as it did when he penned it on his Derry, New Hampshire, farm a century ago. "Something there is that doesn't love a wall / That wants it down." There's a reason that "Mending Wall" is one of the most analyzed and anthologized poems in modern literature; it speaks to our deep human belief in the power of tangible barriers to help us sort, organize, and—ultimately— shield and protect. Yet Frost beautifully illuminates an equally formidable countervailing force within humanity: a mighty desire for connection.

In the poem, he's startled by his neighbor's fierce policing of the wall's durability. "I see him there / Bringing a stone grasped firmly by the top / In each hand, like an old-stone savage armed / He moves in darkness as it seems to me, / Not of woods only and the shade of trees." The darkness of heart that patrols the wall will ever be a barrier to deep connection and understanding.

I've just returned from a trip to the United Kingdom, and my head is chock-full of images of walls, castles, moats, and ruins. I recalled Peter Schneider's 1982 novel *The Wall Jumper* and the absurdity of the bifurcation of Berlin, and I pondered the massive cement fortifications of the Green Zone of Baghdad during the American occupation. There is one thing that the Tower of London, Lowther Castle, the stunning fortifications at Penrith and Carlisle, and Hadrian's Wall near the Scottish border share: they don't work. Through the blur of parapets and palisades and carefully constructed stone walls that I spied from the windows of the old-world pub in little Armathwaite in Cumbria, I kept landing at the same place. We each build emotional barricades and psychological redoubts.

It is easy for me to identify the idiocy and foolishness of Trump's illusory wall. It is much more difficult for me to identify and dismantle the walls that I construct myself. But dismantling the barricades that divide us, living courageously in the face of fear, is the work of adulthood. I'm seeking the bravery and humility to keep taking down my own walls. I fervently hope that we can do so as a nation as well.

The Bear Awakes

§

PRESIDENT GEORGE W. BUSH, at his 2001 summit with Russian president Vladimir Putin, said of his newfound friend, "I looked the man in the eye. I was able to get a sense of his soul." This oft-mocked assessment of Putin—dubbed "Pootie Poot" by the nickname-obsessed W—struck many at the time as naïve but relatively harmless hyperbole. By the time he rolled out his anecdote-laced memoir, *Decision Points,* nine years later, Bush called Putin coldblooded. And now, three years after Bush's reevaluation, we get the full measure of the man. Putin is not just hard-hearted; he governs without any moral compass at all.

Last week, Russian courts convicted anti-corruption blog-ger and opposition leader Alexei Navalny of embezzlement, sentencing him to five years—and barring him from seek-ing any public office in the future. The Kremlin brought false charges against Navalny, like others before him, in order to eliminate any threat to Putin's power. Navalny—who refers to Putin's United Russia Party as the party of "crooks and thieves"—uses his social media savvy to galvanize young followers through his acerbic and pointed tweets. Shrewd and fearless, he's a real threat to Putin's power; he has the ear of the next generation.

Navalny first became a force in Russian politics in 2008 when he blogged about corruption at some of Russia's big state-controlled corporations. As the BBC reported in early July, he became a minority stakeholder in major oil companies, banks, and ministries, and he asked awkward questions about "holes in state finances." He implored Western nations to become vigilant about tracking "dirty money" and challenged them to have the guts to deny visas to those in the ruling party who have cracked down on opposition leaders and activists. For this he faces prison.

Although we often look at our own criminal justice system with a jaundiced eye, our troubles appear less extreme when compared to what Miriam Elder—longtime Russia correspondent for *The Guardian*—refers to as Russia's "Kafkaesque justice system, its torturous prisons, and even its vengeful foreign policy."

Take the absurd case of Sergei Magnitsky, an auditor and lawyer at the Moscow firm Firestone Duncan. Hired to investigate alleged tax evasion at Hermitage Capital Management, he found no wrongdoing at Hermitage, but instead discovered that local officials had pocketed Hermitage's huge tax payments. He reported the corruption and was rewarded by being arrested himself. The thirty-seven-year-old lawyer died in prison in 2009 while awaiting trial after being refused medical treatment—the fate of at least eleven people each day in Russian prisons. In March of 2013, Magnitsky became the first dead man in Russia's history to stand trial.

The US Congress, pressured by William Browder, Magnitsky's former employer, passed the Magnitsky bill, which bars those involved in his death from entering or even keeping bank accounts in the United States. Moscow responded by banning Americans from adopting Russian orphans.

Alexei Nalvany is just the most recent high-profile victim of Putin's unconscionable malice. Putin's targets include: media magnates Vladimir Gusinsky and Boris Berezovsky; former head of the oil company Yukos, Mikhail Khordorkovsky; members of the punk band Pussy Riot; leftwing protest leader, Sergei Udaltsov; Anna Politkovskaya and four other reporters from the opposition newspaper *Novaya Gazeta*, who were murdered; and Alexander Litvinenko, who was hunted down by the KGB while in exile in London and poisoned to death with radioactive polonium. Putin's unremitting vengefulness has made the surreal so horribly real; he is omnipresent and unforgiving. From his push to revive the populist People's Front movement to his scapegoating of gays and his new sweeping censorship and treason laws, Putin has become a caricature of an enraged Russian bear, teeth and claws eternally bared, swatting at suspected enemies everywhere.

I've followed the ruthlessness and cynicism of the Kremlin for years, but I've only just come to understand it on a personal level. Several months ago, I met a Russian woman who works for a pro-democracy NGO. She fled Russia after being personally threatened by KGB operatives who warned her that she will be charged under a new anti-treason law and sentenced to twenty years if she continues to push for democratic reforms. She now continues her critical work in exile. We chat regularly via social media, and I recently asked her what Americans can do to help the courageous activists who do this exceedingly perilous work. She implored me to get the word out: "We want people to know what is happening. People must know the real situation in Russia."

When I asked her about a boycott of the upcoming Sochi Olympics, she responded: "Putin doesn't care about how Russia is viewed on the world stage. What he fears is that more European countries will adopt the Magnitsky Law." William Browder concurs: "We found their Achilles heel. Following the money and freezing the money is by far the most effective tool there is when dealing with kleptocracy."

Talk to your network and any connections you have in Europe. Describe the horrible repression in Russia and urge them to agitate for a Magnitsky bill in their own countries. Like Alexei Navalny, use e-mail and social media to inform the world. Although you might "suffer" from only having dial-up internet service here in Vermont, please employ your relative position of privilege and security to rouse widespread opposition. The Bear awakes.

The Fed's Soothsayer

§

OCTOBER 22, 2013

T HE WHISPER CAMPAIGN against Janet Yellen began long before she was officially nominated to become the Federal Reserve chair—arguably the second-most-powerful position in the country. (My apologies to Vice President Joe Biden.) Last summer, the Obama administration floated three possible replacements for Ben Bernanke: the Fed vice-chair at the time, Yellen; economist and former Fed vice-chair Donald Kohn; and the controversial Laurence Summers. Although Summers quickly rose to the top of the list, President Obama underestimated Democrats' distaste for Summers—who supported deregulation of the banking industry when he served in the Clinton administration.

In a highly unusual move, twenty US senators—our own Bernie Sanders included—drafted a letter in support of a Janet Yellen nomination, signaling that they would not support Summers's confirmation. In September, Sanders released a statement decrying Summers: "What the American people want now is a Fed chairman prepared to stand up to the greed, recklessness, and illegal behavior on Wall Street—not a Wall Street insider." Democrats' public support of Yellen, coupled with the lukewarm reception of Summers by the Republicans on the Senate banking committee, meant that a Summers confirmation would be a tough fight. Summers withdrew his name for consideration, but not before members of his team started a campaign against Yellen.

Ezra Klein of the *Washington Post* and Matthew O'Brien of *The Atlantic* have both written about the subtle sexist attacks on Yellen, which started when some within the Summers camp asserted that Yellen lacked the requisite "gravitas" for the job. They claimed that she lacked the grit or nerve to face a financial crisis. The soft-spoken Bernanke—who came to the Fed chair with considerably less experience than Yellen— did not face similar opposition. O'Brien quips that this may have something to do with his masculine beard, but it most certainly does not have anything to do with his public-speaking strength. According to the Wall Street Journal, Bernanke hired a public-speaking coach to help him make stronger, clearer statements that would not be misinterpreted by the markets; such misinterpretations had been his Achilles heel during his first term.

"Gravitas" aside, Janet Yellen would be "perhaps the most qualified Fed chair in history," according to Dylan Matthews of the *Washington Post's Wonkblog*. Not even highly esteemed economist Paul Volcker—who chaired the Fed under Presidents Carter and Reagan and is credited with ending high levels of inflation—had the experience that Yellen brings to the job. Matthews asserts that Volcker "had nowhere near as much exposure to the highest echelons of the Fed system as Yellen has." More importantly, by the *Wall Street Journal's* analysis Yellen's record of predictions is better than that of any of her Fed colleagues in recent years. She was one of the few at the Fed who accurately predicted that the subprime crisis was not over in 2007 and that the United States was in real danger of a credit crunch and subsequent recession—exactly as indeed came to pass in 2008.

So, what gives? If she's supremely qualified and highly respected, and is an economic soothsayer, why the resistance to Yellen's nomination? Jena McGregor of the *Washington Post's* online column *On Leadership* teases out reasons in a recent post. McGregor points out that new studies show that although women leaders, who used to be penalized for assertiveness, now have more freedom to be bold and decisive without being penalized, yet another double bind for women has emerged. A paper in the British *Journal of Social Psychology* describes a study in which women leaders were penalized for not demonstrating assertive, forceful behaviors, while male leaders were given permission not to. McGregor concludes, "In other words, they're damned if they do and doomed if they don't."

This "gravitas" drama reminds me of two other memorable nominations. Remember when George W. Bush floated the idea of nominating White House counsel Harriet Miers to succeed retiring Supreme Court justice Sandra Day O'Connor? Conservatives howled because the dark horse Miers did not have a public conservative track record. But I felt indignant about her nomination because there were so many other supremely qualified right-leaning women candidates: Karen Williams, Alice Batchelder, Maura Corrigan, and Maureen Mahoney among them. He seemed to have picked Miers because she was a decent lawyer who would be loyal to the Bush Doctrine, the foreign policy principle of using unilateralism and pre-emptive strikes to combat terrorism. By passing over much more qualified female legal minds with considerable constitutional law experience, Bush was signaling that any woman would do.

I had the same feeling when John McCain tapped Sarah Palin, a rookie governor with very little experience or track record, to be his running mate in the 2008 presidential contest. Granted, there are many factors involved in a vice presidential pick, but Sarah Palin was the only woman on McCain's short list. He didn't seriously consider accomplished GOP women like Christie Todd Whitman, Kay Baily Hutchinson, Olympia Snowe, or Jodi Rell. It's hard not to believe that he wanted a "trophy" candidate in much the same way that some older men seek to marry beautiful young women. If this sounds harsh, consider what McCain quipped multiple times when female US senators took the initiative last week to end the government shutdown: "The women are taking over." (Women still make up only one-fifth of the upper chamber of Congress.) Len Burman, a former colleague of Yellen's in the Clinton Administration, recently wrote about his overwhelmingly positive experience of working with Yellen: "Imagine having a Fed chair who is not only brilliant and persuasive, but also modest. Imagine a Fed chair who could build consensus, who would not leave colleagues feeling they have been browbeaten or berated, but rather persuaded. If she makes a decision they disagree with, they won't feel disrespected."

I'll take brilliance and collegiality over "gravitas" any day.

No Time for Timidity

§

DECEMBER 29, 2017

PAUL WELLSTONE, the US senator from Minnesota who died in a plane crash in 2002, is well known for his stirring adage, "We all do better when we all do better." But there's another Wellstone pearl that's become my clarion: "This is no time for timidity."

This line calls to me as I reflect upon an excruciating year in which we witnessed terrific dysfunction and a tremendous meanness of spirit and strategy. It also guides me as I contemplate the horrible twists and turns sure to come and helps me to stave off feelings of doom and paralysis. It points me towards usefulness and away from feeling useless, and it awakens a hopefulness that has been slumbering fitfully.

Since Trump's ascendancy, my brother-in-law has decided to focus his energy as a way to counteract creeping despondency. Fighting racism in America has become his most important issue, so he's spending his time and money to get more people of color elected to higher office. He's backing a

Democratic congressional candidate in his home district and following many other US House races across the country.

A former coach, he's no longer content merely to watch the court from the sidelines; now he's offering suggestions to his chosen candidate's team so they can make their candidate's social media presence more powerful and effective. Simply, he's become absolutely engaged in the process of changing the face of politics in this country.

He believes, as I do, that we all have a part to play in the great struggle for a more just and gentle world. And as the year turns, I'll plan concrete actions of my own to bring about that change.

How will you, too, become more fully engaged in transforming the world? What can you bring to this all-important task? Will you offer a sharp mind? Time? A meeting space? Money? Editing skills? Communications acumen? Plenty of energy and positivity? Fierce loyalty, compassion?

Are you a connector? An excellent researcher? Are you an artist? A performer? A great organizer of people, places, or things? Do you move people with your music, your food, your words? Do you have a big heart that's searching for a landing place? Or do you have a healthy skepticism that can coax us all towards greatness?

My call to action is expansive, inclusive, and absolutely urgent. It's well past time for all of us to put down our insecurities; they are serving no good master. Push yourself beyond simply caring (and worrying); it's time to *do*.

I understand that the *doing* feels pointless at times. The world is immense and complicated and often feels like a great big mess. What impact do our relatively small actions truly have on anything at all? Perhaps this is actually the wrong question—the wrong frame entirely—for understanding our predicament.

The actions themselves, regardless of grand outcomes, are the point. The process of meaning-making—of crafting culture and creating connections—is the heart of it all. We're living through a deeply troubling time in history, and many of us feel trapped in someone else's narrative. But the meaning makers, the history shapers, are not the people at the top. It's the rest of us. As a historian, I know this to be true.

The sycophants—and the "yes" men and women—grab the headlines, sure. But historians will look to the rest of us and our response to the insanity. I tell you, this is no time for timidity. Because this horrible moment in time is not just about us. It's about our children and the generations that come after who will want to know: What did you do to fight the darkness?

Notes

§

Part 1

Framingham Heart Study. https://framinghamheartstudy.org (last visited March 20, 2022).

Gilbert, Elizabeth, "Your Elusive Creative Genius" TED Talk, February, 2009. https://www.ted.com.

Hill, Napoleon, *Think and Grow Rich*, The Ralston Society, 1937.

Juvonen, Jaana, "Bullying Among Sixth Graders a Daily Occurence," *Science Daily*, April 11, 2005. https://www.sciencedaily.com/releases /2005/04/050411100940.htm (last visited March 20, 2022).

Martin, Douglas, "Ulrich Neisser is Dead at 83, Reshaped Study of the Mind" *New York Times*, Feb. 25, 2012.

Wheeler, Cheryl, "I'm Unworthy," Penrod And Higgins Music/Amachrist Music, ACF Music Group International. Copyright reserved, May, 20, 1997. www.cherylwheeler.com

Winthrop University, "N.Y. Times Details English Chair Gregg Heci-movich's Work on Identifying Slave Author," *Winthrop News* 2013. https://digitalcommons.winthrop.edu/winthropnews2013/185Part 1

Part 4

Brown, Brene, *The Anatomy of Trust*, Super Soul Sessions. https:// brenebrown.com/videos/anatomy-trust-video/2015 (last visited on March 21, 2022).

Kubzansky, Laura, "Happiness and Health," *Harvard Public Health*, Winter 2011. https://www.hsph.harvard.edu/news/magazine/happiness-stress-heart-disease/ (last visited March 21, 2022).

Part 5

Brooks, Gwendolyn, "Paul Robeson," *The Essential Gwendolyn Brooks,* Library of America, 2005. Copyright © 1970 by Gwendolyn Brooks.

DuBois, W.E.B., "The Talented Tenth," from *The Negro Problem: A Series of Articles by Representative Negroes of Today,* New York, 1903.

Goldberg, Jonah, "On the GOP Menu for 2012," *National Review Online,* Nov. 2011. https://www.nationalreview.com/2011/03/gop-menu-2012-jonah-goldberg/ (last visited March 21, 2022).

Part 6

Baldwin, Neil, "There's a 1,200 year old Phone in the Smithsonian Collections," *Smithsonian Magazine,* Dec. 2013.

Bethell, Tom, "Blasphemous Chic," *American Spectator,* Aug. 22, 2012.

Blow, Charles, "Beyond the Courtroom," *New York Times,* July 10, 2013.

Borger, Julian, "Bush's Love of Pootie-Poot Putin," *The Guardian,* May 19, 2002.

Bush, George, W., *Decision Points,* Crown Publishing Group. Nov. 2010.

Carlson, Marta, *Das Pow Wow: Deconstructing German Caricature of American Indians,* Volume 99, Part 2000, American Anthropological Association.

Cohen, Nick, "An evil collusion between a tyrant and a man of God," *The Guardian,* Aug. 18, 2012.

"Conspiracy theories are dangerous—here's how to crush them," *The Economist,* Aug. 12, 2019.

Day, Gordon, M., "Oral Tradition as a Complement," *Ethnohistory 19/2,* Spring 1972.

DeLoria, Philip, *Indians in Unexpected Places,* University Press of Kansas, Oct. 2004.

Esler, Gavin, "Germans can't escape their Lutheran past," *BBC,* March 25, 2012. https://www.bbc.com/news/magazine-17489035 (last visited April 12, 2022).

Langguth, Gerd, *Angela Merkel,* DTV, Oct. 30, 2005.

Lynch, Michael, "Teaching Humility in an Age of Arrogance," *The Chronicle of Higher Education,* June 5, 2012.

Matthews, Dylan, "Nine amazing facts about Janet Yellen, our next Fed Chair," *Washington Post*, Wonkblog, Oct. 9, 2013.

McGregor, Jena, "Janet Yellen's Leadership style is right for the Fed and for the future," *Washington Post*, On Leadership, Oct. 9, 2013.

Mitchell, Anais, *Hadestown*, Samuel French Publishing, May 21, 2021.

Rosenblum, Nancy L., and Russell Muirhead, *A Lot of People are Saying: The New Conspiracism and the Assault on Democracy*, Princeton University Press, 2019.

Schneider, Peter, *The Wall Jumper*, University of Chicago Press, Nov. 1, 1998.

Tippett, Krista, "This history is long, This history is deep" an interview with Isabel Wilkerson, *On Being*, National Public Radio. Original Air Date, Nov. 17, 2016.

Warner, Jeremy, "Angela Merkel isn't bluffing; like everyone else in Europe she's defending national sovereignty," *The Telegraph*, June 27, 2012.

Acknowledgments

§

WHEN I STARTED thinking about putting my articles together into a book, I thought it would be easy because all the writing had already been done. Little did I know! The process of finding, reading through, weeding out, and editing the hundreds of articles written over almost ten years became daunting at times. Jerry Carbone deployed his librarian know-how to locate columns I had given up for lost, finding them in the nooks and crannies of the Internet. I am grateful for the support of my spouse, Elizabeth, and my friends Ella Spottswood and Chloe Learey for tackling these nitty gritty tasks with me and helping to keep the project on track. And a big shout-out to my editor, Mike Fleming, for bringing all the pieces together, and for being patient over several years of fits and starts.

I am awed by the incredible work of Dede Cummings and the remarkable staff at Green Writers Press who took my ideas and made this beautiful book you are holding in your hands.

I cannot thank my friend, mentor, and coach Laura Coyle enough. When my dream of running for office had burned down to a tiny ember, she blew gently on it, encouraging me to start writing and submitting work every once in a while.

Many thanks to Bob Audette of the *Brattleboro Reformer* and writer Becky Karush for getting me started on writing a weekly column in the first place, and to the many readers who gave feedback over the years and helped the column and my thinking evolve.

I am also grateful for the people in these pages, from the grizzled guys to Madame No, who gave me the opportunity to reflect and learn through my writing. I deeply appreciate the lessons that others have to offer, including those with whom we disagree.

About the Author

§

ECCA BALINT is a Vermont State Senator from
Windham County, the first openly gay woman to
serve in the Vermont Senate. She was elected majority
leader by the Democratic caucus in 2016, and President Pro
Tempore in 2020. She has been an educator in many different
settings, from summer camp to middle school to community
college, working with people of all ages and backgrounds.

Becca is a fierce advocate for justice and equity, and her
values were shaped by her family's experiences. She's the
daughter of an immigrant dad and a working-class mom,
and her parents never took for granted the rights and privileges provided by the United States Constitution. Her paternal grandfather was killed in the Holocaust, and her father's
family saw firsthand the cruelties people can perpetrate when
the law does not protect minorities, or when the government
approves the targeting of those who are seen as different.

Becca lives in Brattleboro with her wife, two children, and
a labradoodle named Wheelie.